Homer
The Odyssey
Abridged

Third Edition

Translated
by
Ian Johnston
Vancouver Island University
Nanaimo, British Columbia,
Canada

Richer Resources Publications
Arlington Virginia
USA

Homer
The Odyssey Abridged

Cover Art by Ian Crowe

The full text of this volume is available for download on the web at:

http://www.mala.bc.ca/~johnstoi/homer/iliad_title.htm

Reprint requests and requests for additional copies of this book can be addressed to

Richer Resources Publications
1926 N. Woodrow Street
Arlington, Virginia 22207

or via our website at:
www.RicherResourcesPublications.com

ISBN 978-0-9818162-9-6
Library of Congress Control Number 2008932226

Published by Richer Resources Publications
Arlington, Virginia, USA

TABLE OF CONTENTS

[Books in square brackets have been omitted entirely]

Translator's Note

This abridged text of Homer's *Odyssey* has been prepared by Ian Johnston of Vancouver Island University, Nanaimo, BC, Canada, from his translation of the full text, available on line or as a published paperback book from Richer Resources Publications. The abridged text is about one third the length of the original.

In this abridged version, every line is a translation from Homer's text, except for a very few short phrases inserted as transitions. At times I have included a brief summary statement describing some missing material. These are in brackets and italics. Such insertions are meant to maintain the continuity of the abridged narrative, not to describe all the material which has been omitted.

In numbering the lines, the translator has normally included a short indented line with the line immediately above, so that the two short lines count as a single line in the reckoning. There are some exceptions to this practice.

This Third Edition of the abridged *Odyssey* is almost identical to the other editions. The text has been re-formatted to fit a slightly larger page, a few lines have been added, some errors have been corrected, and line numbers of the Greek text have been added (these are in square brackets to the right of the text).

BOOK ONE

I

ATHENA VISITS ITHACA

Muse, speak to me now of that resourceful man
who wandered far and wide after ravaging
the sacred citadel of Troy.[1] He came to see
many people's cities, where he learned their customs,
while on the sea his spirit suffered many torments,
as he fought to save his life and lead his comrades home.
But though he wanted to, he could not rescue them—
they all died from their own stupidity, the fools.
They feasted on the cattle of Hyperion,
god of the sun—that's why he snatched away their chance   10
of getting home someday. So now, daughter of Zeus,
tell us his story, starting anywhere you wish.   [10]

The other warriors, all those who had escaped
being utterly destroyed, were now back safely home,
facing no more dangers from battle or the sea.
But Odysseus, who longed to get back to his wife
and reach his home, was being held in a hollow cave
by that mighty nymph Calypso, noble goddess,
who wished to make Odysseus her husband.
But as the seasons came and went, the year arrived   20
in which, according to what gods had once ordained,
he was to get back to Ithaca, his home—
not that he would be free from troubles even there,
among his family. The gods pitied Odysseus,   [20]
all except Poseidon, who kept up his anger
against godlike Odysseus and did not relent
until he reached his native land.

                But at that moment,
Poseidon was among the Ethiopians,
a long way off. But other gods had gathered
in the great hall of Olympian Zeus. Among them all,   30
the father of gods and men was first to speak.
In his heart he was remembering royal Aegisthus,
whom Orestes, Agamemnon's famous son,
had killed. With him in mind, Zeus addressed the gods:

---

[1]The Muses, the divine patrons of the arts, are daughters of Zeus.

"It's disgraceful how these humans blame the gods.
They say their tribulations come from us,
when they themselves, through their own foolishness,
bring hardships which are not decreed by Fate.
Now there's Aegisthus, who took for himself
the wife of Agamemnon, Atreus' son,   40
and then murdered him, once the man came home.[1]
None of that was set by Fate. Aegisthus knew
his acts would bring on his total ruin.
For Orestes would avenge the son of Atreus,
once he grew up and longed for his own land.   [40]
So he has paid for everything in full."

Athena, goddess with the gleaming eyes, answered Zeus:

"Son of Cronos and father to us all,
you who rule on high, yes indeed, Aegisthus
now lies dead, something he well deserved.   50
May any other man who does what he did
also be destroyed! But my heart is torn
for skillful Odysseus, ill-fated man,
who has had to suffer such misfortune
for so many years, a long way from friends.
He's on an island, surrounded by the sea,
the one that forms the ocean's navel stone.[2]   [50]
In the forests of that island lives a goddess,
who stops the sad, unlucky man from leaving.
But Odysseus yearns to see even the smoke   60
rising from his native land and longs
for death. And yet, Olympian Zeus, your heart
does not respond to him. Did not Odysseus   [60]
offer you delightful sacrifices
on Troy's far-reaching plain beside the ships?
Why then, Zeus, are you so angry with him?"

Cloud-gatherer Zeus then answered her and said:

---

[1] Aegisthus had seduced Agamemnon's wife, Clytaemnestra, while Agamemnon was fighting in Troy, and, when he returned from the war, the two lovers murdered Agamemnon and took control of Argos. Orestes, who was away at the time, came back to Argos in disguise and avenged his father. This famous story is referred to a number of times in the *Odyssey*.

[2] The Greek word *omphalos* (navel stone) Homer uses here to describe Calypso's island of Ogygia.

"My child,
what a speech has passed the barrier of your teeth!
How could I forget godlike Odysseus,
preeminent among all mortal men   70
for his intelligence and offerings
to the immortal gods, who hold wide heaven?
But Earthshaker Poseidon is a stubborn god,
constantly enraged about the cyclops,
the one whose eye Odysseus destroyed,
Still, he has no plans to kill him. But come,
let's all of us consider his return,
so he can journey back to Ithaca.
Poseidon's anger will relent. He can't
fight the immortal gods all by himself,   80
not with all of us opposing him."

Goddess Athena with the gleaming eyes replied to Zeus: [80]

"Son of Cronos and father to us all,
ruling high above, if the immortal gods
now find it pleasing for the wise Odysseus
to return back home, then let's send Hermes,
killer of Argus, as our messenger,
over to the island of Ogygia,
so he can quickly tell that fair-haired nymph
our firm decision—that brave Odysseus   90
will now leave and complete his voyage home.[1]
I'll go to Ithaca and urge his son
to be more active, put courage in his heart,
so he will call those long-haired Achaeans   [90]
to assembly, and there address the suitors,
who keep on slaughtering his flocks of sheep
and shambling bent-horned cattle.[2] I'll send him
on a trip to Sparta and sandy Pylos,
to learn about his father's voyage home—
he may hear of it somewhere—and to gain   100
a worthy reputation among men."

---

[1] The god Hermes, a son of Zeus, killed the monster Argus, whom Hera had told to guard the goddess Io, to prevent her getting into sexual mischief with Zeus. Hermes acted on Zeus' instructions.

[2] The suitors are the rich young aristocratic men of Ithaca and the islands who are seeking to marry Penelope, Odysseus' wife, in the belief that Odysseus is dead.

Athena spoke. Then she tied those lovely sandals
on her feet, the immortal, golden sandals
which carry her as fast as stormy blasts of wind
across the ocean seas and endless tracts of land.
She raced down from the peak of Mount Olympus,
sped across to Ithaca, and then just stood there,
at Odysseus' outer gate before the palace,
on the threshold, gripping a bronze spear in her fist.
She looked like Mentes, a foreigner, the chief   110
who ruled the Taphians. There she met the suitors,
those arrogant men, who were enjoying themselves
playing checkers right outside the door, sitting down
on hides of cattle.

                    Godlike Telemachus
observed Athena first, well before the others.
He moved up near Athena, then he spoke to her—
his words had wings:

          "Welcome to you stranger.
You must enjoy our hospitality.
Then, after you have had some food to eat,
you can tell us what you need."

                    Saying this,   120
Telemachus led Pallas Athena into his home.
He brought Athena in and sat her in a chair,
a beautifully crafted work. Under it   [130]
he rolled out a linen mat and then arranged
a foot stool for her feet. Beside her he drew up
a lovely decorated chair for him to sit in.
A female servant carried in a fine gold jug
and poured water out into a silver basin,
so they could wash their hands. Beside them she set down
a polished table. Then the worthy housekeeper   130
brought in the bread and set it down before them.
Next, she laid out a wide variety of food,
drawing freely on supplies she had in store.   [140]
A carver sliced up many different cuts of meat
and served them. He set out goblets made of gold,
as a herald went back and forth pouring their wine.

Then, one after another, the proud suitors came.
They sat down on reclining seats and high-backed chairs.
Heralds poured water out for them to wash their hands,

and women servants piled some baskets full of bread,   140
while young lads filled their bowls up to the brim with drink.
The suitors reached out with their hands to grab
the tasty food prepared and placed in front of them.
When each and every man had satisfied his need   [150]
for food and drink, their hearts craved something more—
dancing and song—the finest joys of dinner feasts.
A herald gave a splendid lyre to Phemius,
so he was forced to sing in front of all the suitors.
On the strings he plucked the prelude to a lovely song.
But then Telemachus, leaning his head over   150
close to Athena, so no one else could listen,
murmured to her:

         "Dear stranger, my guest,
if I tell you something, will I upset you?
These men here, they spend all their time like this,
with songs and music—it's so easy for them,
because they gorge themselves on what belongs   [160]
to someone else, and with impunity,
a man whose white bones now may well be lying
on the mainland somewhere, rotting in the rain,
or in the sea, being tossed around by waves.   160
If they saw him return to Ithaca,
they'd all be praying they had swifter feet
rather than more wealth in gold or clothes.
But by now some evil fate has killed him,
and for us there is no consolation,
not even if some earthbound mortal man
should say that he will come. But tell me,
and speak candidly—Who are your people?
What city do you come from?

               Then Athena,
goddess with the gleaming eyes, answered Telemachus: 170

"To you I will indeed speak openly.
I can tell you that my name is Mentes,   [180]
son of the wise Anchialus, and king
of the oar-loving Taphians. My ship
is berthed some distance from the city.
But come, speak openly and tell me this—
What is this feast? Who are these crowds of men?
Why do you need this? Is it a wedding?
Or a drinking party? It seems clear enough

this is no meal where each man brings his share.   180
It strikes me that these men are acting here
in an insulting, overbearing way,
while dining in your home."

                Noble Telemachus   [230]
then said to Athena in reply:

                      "Stranger,
since you've questioned me about the matter,
I'll tell you. Our house was once well on its way
to being rich and famous—at that time
Odysseus was alive among his people.
But now the gods with their malicious plans
have changed all that completely. They make sure   190
Odysseus stays where nobody can see him—
they've not done this to anyone before.
But it's not him alone who makes me sad
and cry out in distress. For now the gods
have brought me other grievous troubles.
All the best young men who rule the islands,
Dulichium and wooded Zacynthus,
and Same, as well as those who lord it here
in rocky Ithaca—they are all now
wooing my mother and ravaging my house.[1]   200
She won't turn down a marriage she detests,
but can't bring herself to make the final choice.
Meanwhile, these men are feasting on my home   [250]
and soon will be the death of me as well."

This made Pallas Athena angry—she said to him:

"It's bad Odysseus has wandered off
when you need him here so much! He could lay
his hands upon these shameless suitors.
Listen now to what I'm going to tell you.
Tomorrow you must call Achaea's warriors   210
to an assembly and address them all,
appealing to the gods as witnesses.
Tell the suitors to return to their own homes.
As for your mother, if her heart is set

---

[1]Dulichium, Zacynthus, and Same are islands close to Ithaca, part of Odysseus'
kingdom.

on getting married, then let her return
to where her father lives, for he's a man
of power with great capabilities.
He'll organize the marriage and arrange
the wedding gifts, as many as befit
a well-loved daughter. Now, as for yourself,   220
if you'll listen, I have some wise advice.
Set off in search of news about your father,
who's been gone so long. Some living mortal
may tell you something, or you may hear
a voice from Zeus, which often brings men news.
Sail first to Pylos—speak to noble Nestor.
After you've been there, proceed to Sparta
and fair-haired Menelaus, the last one
of all bronze-clad Achaeans to get home.
You must not keep on acting like a child—   230
the time has come when you're too old for that.

Prudent Telemachus then answered her:

"Stranger, you've been speaking as a friend,
thinking as a father would for his own son—
and what you've said I never will forget.
But come now, though you're eager to be off,
stay here a while. Once you've had a bath   [310]
and your fond heart is fully satisfied,
then go back to your ship with your spirit
full of joy, carrying a costly present,   240
something really beautiful, which will be
my gift to you, an heirloom of the sort
dear guest-friends give to those who are their friends."

Goddess Athena with the gleaming eyes then said to him:

"Since I'm eager to depart, don't keep me here
a moment longer. And whatever gift
your heart suggests you give me as a friend,
present it to me when I come back here,
and pick me something truly beautiful.
It will earn you something worthy in return."   250

This said, Athena with the gleaming eyes departed,
flying off like some wild sea bird. In his heart she put   [320]
courage and strength. She made him recall his father,
even more so than before. In his mind, Telemachus
pictured her, and his heart was full of wonder.

11

He thought she was a god. So he moved away.
And then the noble youth rejoined the suitors.
Celebrated Phemius was performing for them,
as they sat in silence, listening. He was singing
of the return of the Achaeans, that bitter trip   260
Athena made them take sailing home from Troy.

In her upper room, the daughter of Icarius,
wise Penelope, heard the man's inspired song.
She came down the towering staircase from her room,   [330]
but not alone—two female servants followed her.
When beautiful Penelope reached the suitors,
she stayed beside the door post in the well-built room,
with a small, bright veil across her face. On either side
her two attendants stood. With tears streaming down,
Penelope addressed the famous singer:

           "Phemius,   270
you know all sorts of other ways to charm
an audience, actions of gods and men
which singers celebrate. As you sit here,
sing one of those, while these men drink their wine
in silence. Don't keep up that painful song,   [340]
which always breaks the heart here in my chest,
for, more than anyone, I am weighed down
with ceaseless grief which I cannot forget.
I always remember with such yearning
my husband's face, a man whose fame has spread   280
far and wide through Greece and central Argos."

Sensible Telemachus answered her and said:

"Mother, why begrudge the faithful singer
delighting us in any way his mind
may prompt him? One cannot blame the singers.
It seems to me it's Zeus' fault. He hands out
to toiling men, each and every one of them,
whatever he desires. There's nothing wrong
with this man's singing of the evil fate   [350]
of the Danaans, for men praise the most   290
the song which they have heard most recently.
Your heart and spirit should endure his song.
For Odysseus was not the only man
at Troy who lost his chance to see the day
he would come back. Many men were killed.

12

Go up to your rooms and keep busy there
with your own work, the spindle and the loom.
Tell your servants to perform their duties.
Talking is a man's concern, every man's,
but especially mine, since in this house   300
I'm the one in charge."

          Astonished at his words,   [360]
Penelope went back to her own chambers,
setting in her heart the prudent words her son had said.
With her attendant women she climbed the stairs
up to her rooms and there wept for Odysseus,
her dear husband, until bright-eyed Athena
cast sweet sleep upon her eyelids.

          In the shadowy halls
the suitors started to create an uproar,
each man shouting out his hope to lie beside her.
Then shrewd Telemachus began his speech to them: 310

"You suitors of my mother, who all have
such insolent arrogance, let us for now
enjoy our banquet. But no more shouting,
for it's grand to listen to a singer   [370]
as fine as this one—his voice is like a god's.
Then in the morning let us all assemble,
sit down for a meeting, so I can speak
and tell you firmly to depart my home.
Make yourself some different meals which eat up
your own possessions, moving house to house.   320
But if you think it's preferable and better
for one man's livelihood to be consumed
without paying anything, I'll call upon
the immortal gods to see if Zeus
will bring about an act of retribution.
And if you are destroyed inside my home,   [380]
you will not be avenged."

          Telemachus finished.
They all bit their lips, astonished at the boldness
in his words. Then, Antinous, son of Eupeithes,
declared:

          "Telemachus, the gods themselves,   330
it seems, are teaching you to be a braggart
and give rash speeches. I do hope that Zeus,

son of Cronos, does not make you king
of this sea island Ithaca, even though
it is your father's legacy to you."

                  At that point, the suitors
switched to dancing and to singing lovely songs.
They amused themselves until dark evening came.
Then each man went to his own house to sleep.
Telemachus moved up to where his room was built,
high in the splendid courtyard, with a spacious view,   340
his mind much preoccupied on his way to bed.
Accompanying him, quick-minded Eurycleia
held two flaming torches. She was Ops' daughter.
Of all the female household slaves she was the one
who loved him most, for she had nursed him as a child.
He opened the doors of the well-constructed room,
sat on the bed, and pulled off his soft tunic,
handed it to the wise old woman, who smoothed it out,
and folded it, then hung the tunic on a peg
beside the corded bedstead. Then she left the room,   350 [440]
pulling the door shut by its silver handle.
Telemachus lay there all night long, wrapped up
in sheep's wool, his mind thinking of the journey
which Athena had earlier proposed to him.

BOOK TWO

II

TELEMACHUS PREPARES FOR HIS VOYAGE

As soon as rose-fingered early Dawn appeared,
Odysseus' dear son jumped up out of bed and dressed.
He slung a sharp sword from his shoulders, then laced
his lovely sandals over his shining feet.
At once he asked the loud-voiced heralds to summon
all the long-haired Achaeans to assembly.
They issued the call, and the Achaeans came,
gathering quickly. When the assembly had convened,
Telemachus moved to the meeting. Among the men   [10]
heroic Aegyptius was the first to speak,   10
an old man stooped with age,

             "Men of Ithaca,
listen now to what I have to say.
We have not held a general meeting
or assembly since the day Odysseus
sailed off in his hollow ships. What man
has made us gather now? What's his reason?
Has he heard some news about the army   [30]
and will tell us details of its journey home,
or is it some other public business
he will introduce and talk about?"   20

Odysseus' dear son Telemachus began to speak,
talking to Aegyptius first of all:

                    "Old man,   [40]
the one who called the people to this meeting
is not far off, as you will quickly learn.
I did. For I'm a man who suffers more
than other men. But I have no reports
of our returning army, no details
I've just heard myself to pass along to you,
nor is there other public business
I'll announce or talk about. The issue here   30
is my own need, for on my household
troubles have fallen in a double sense.
First, my noble father's perished, the man
who was once your king and my kind father.
And then there's an even greater problem,
which will quickly and completely shatter
this entire house, and my whole livelihood

will be destroyed. These suitors, the dear sons [50]
of those men here with most nobility,
are pestering my mother against her will. 40
They don't want to journey to her father,
Icarius, in his home, where he himself
could set a bride price for his daughter
and give her to the man he feels he likes,
the one who pleases him the most. Instead,
they hang around our house, day after day,
slaughtering oxen, fat goats, and sheep.
They keep on feasting, drinking sparkling wine
without restraint, and they consume so much.
My home is being demolished in a way 50
that is not right. You men should be ashamed."

Telemachus spoke, then threw the sceptre on the ground [80]
and burst out crying. Everyone there pitied him,
so all the other men kept silent, unwilling
to give an angry answer to Telemachus.
Antinous was the only one to speak. He said:

"Telemachus you boaster, your spirit
is too unrestrained. How you carry on,
trying to shame us, since you so desire
the blame should rest on us. But in your case, 60
Achaean suitors aren't the guilty ones.
Your own dear mother is, who understands
how to use deceit. It's been three years now—
and soon it will be four—since she began
to frustrate hearts in our Achaean chests. [90]
She gives hope to each of us, makes promises
to everyone, and sends out messages.
But her intent is different. In her mind
she has thought up another stratagem:
in her room she had a large loom set up, 70
and started weaving something very big,
with thread that was quite thin. She said to us:

'Young men, those of you who are my suitors,
since lord Odysseus is dead, you must wait,
although you're keen for me to marry,
till I complete this cloak—otherwise
my weaving would be wasted and in vain.
It is a shroud for warrior Laertes,
for the day a lethal fate will strike him. [100]

16

Then none of the Achaean women here   80
will be annoyed with me because a man
who acquired so many rich possessions
should lie without a shroud.'

           "That's what she said.
And our proud hearts agreed. And so each day
she wove at her great loom, but every night
she set up torches and pulled the work apart.
Three years she fooled Achaeans with this trick.
They trusted her. But as the seasons passed,
the fourth year came. Then one of her women
who knew all the details spoke about them,   90
and we caught her undoing her lovely work.
Thus, we forced her to complete the cloak   [110]
against her will. The suitors now say this,
so you, deep in your heart, will understand
and all Achaeans know—send your mother back.
Tell her she must marry whichever man
her father tells her and who pleases her.
But we are not going back to our own lands,
or some place else, not until she marries
an Achaean man of her own choosing."   100

Prudent Telemachus then said in reply:

"Antinous, there's no way I will dismiss   [130]
out of this house against her will the one
who bore and nursed me. As for my father,
he's in a distant land, alive or dead.
It would be hard for me to compensate
Icarius with a suitable amount,
as I would have to do, if I sent her back.
If I didn't do that, then her father
would treat me badly, and some deity   110
would send other troubles, since my mother,
as she left this house, would call upon
the dreaded Furies.[1] Men would blame me, too.
That's why I'll never issue such an order.
Just give me a swift ship and twenty rowers—
so I can make a journey and return
to various places, to sandy Pylos

---

[1]The Furies are the fearful goddess of blood revenge, especially within the family.

and then to Sparta, to see if I can find
some news about my father's voyage home.
If I hear my father is still living   120
and returning home, I could hold out here
for one more year, although it's hard for me.
If I learn he's dead and gone, I'll come back   [220]
to my dear native land, build him a tomb,
and there perform as many funeral rites
as are appropriate. And after that,
I'll give my mother to a husband."

Telemachus said this and soon dissolved the meeting.
The men dispersed, each man to his own house.

Telemachus walked away to the ocean shore.   130 [260]
There, once he'd washed his hands in grey salt water,
to Athena he made this prayer:

                                "O hear me,
you who yesterday came to my home
as a god and ordered me to set out
on board ship across the murky seas,
to learn about my father's voyage back
after being away so long. All this
Achaeans are preventing, most of all,
the suitors with their wicked arrogance."

As he said this prayer, Athena came up close to him,   140
looking and sounding just like Mentor. She spoke—
her words had wings:

                                "You must not delay
that trip you wish to make. I am a friend
of your ancestral home, so much so that I
will furnish a fast ship for you and come
in person with you. But now you must go home.
Mingle with the suitors. I'll go through the town
and quickly round up a group of comrades,
all volunteers. In sea-girt Ithaca,
I'll choose from the many ships, new and old,   150
the best one for you, and then, when that ship
has been made ready and is fit to sail,
we'll launch it out into the wine-dark sea."

BOOK TWO

*[Telemachus goes down into the storage rooms of the palace and
tells the slave Eurycleia to get some supplies ready for his voyage.
He swears her to secrecy.]*

Telemachus went up into the dining hall
and there rejoined the company of suitors.

Then goddess Athena with the gleaming eyes
thought of something else. Looking like Telemachus,
she went all through the city. To every man
she came across she gave the same instructions,
telling them to meet by the fast ship that evening.   160
Next, she asked Noemon, fine son of Phronius,
for a swift ship, and he was happy to oblige.
Then the sun went down, and all the roads grew dark.
Athena dragged the fast ship down into the sea
and stocked it with supplies, all the materials   [390]
well-decked boats have stowed on board, then moved the ship
to the harbour's outer edge. There they assembled,
that group of brave companions, and the goddess
instilled fresh spirit in every one of them.
Then bright-eyed Athena told Telemachus   170
to come outside, by the entrance to the spacious hall.   [400]
In her voice and form she resembled Mentor:

"Telemachus, your well-armed companions
are already sitting beside their oars,
waiting for you to launch the expedition.
Let's be off, so we don't delay the trip
a moment longer."

        With these words, Pallas Athena
quickly led the way, and Telemachus followed.
Then, with Athena going on board ahead of him,
Telemachus embarked. She sat in the stern.   180
Telemachus sat right beside her, as the men
untied the stern ropes, then climbed aboard the ship
and went to seat themselves beside their oarlocks.
Bright-eyed Athena arranged a fair breeze for them,   [420]
a strong West Wind blowing across the wine-dark sea.
As the ship sliced straight through the swell on its way forward,
around the bow began the great song of the waves.
Then all night long and well beyond the sunrise,
their ship continued sailing on its journey.

BOOK FOUR

III

TELEMACHUS VISITS NESTOR IN PYLOS

[Telemachus and his crew reach Pylos and are welcomed and enter-
tained by Nestor, king of Pylos; Nestor provides a chariot for
Telemachus to journey to Sparta and sends his son Peisistratus
with him on the trip.]

IV

THE SUITORS PLAN TO KILL TELEMACHUS

[Telemachus and Peisistratus reach Menelaus' home in Sparta;
Menelaus gives a long account of his travels in Egypt, especially his
adventures with the Old Man of the Sea, the death of the lesser
Ajax, and the death of Agamemnon; Menelaus invites Telemachus
to stay, but Telemachus declines.]

Meanwhile, back in Telemachus' Ithaca,
the suitors were outside Odysseus' palace,
enjoying themselves by throwing spears and discus
on level ground in front—with all the arrogance
they usually displayed. Their two leaders,
Antinous and handsome Eurymachus,
were sitting there—by far the best of all the suitors.   [630]
Then Noemon, Phronius' son, came up
to question Antinous. He said:

           "Antinous,
  in our hearts do we truly know or not   10
  when Telemachus will be coming back
  from sandy Pylos? He went away
  taking a ship of mine which I now need
  to make the trip across to spacious Elis."

He finished. In their hearts the suitors were amazed.
They had no idea Telemachus had gone
to Pylos, land of Neleus, and still believed
he was somewhere with the flocks on his estates.
Antinous, Eupeithes' son, then spoke to them.   [660]
He was annoyed, his black heart filled with rage,   20
his flashing eyes a fiery blaze:

           "Here's trouble.
  In his overbearing way Telemachus,
  with this voyage of his, has now achieved
  significant success. And we believed

he'd never see it through. Come now,
give me a swift ship and twenty comrades,
so I can watch for him and set an ambush,   [670]
as he navigates his passage through the strait
dividing Ithaca from rugged Samos,
and bring this trip searching for his father   30
to a dismal end."

                Antinous picked out his men,
twenty of the best. They went down to the shore
and dragged a swift black ship into deep water.   [780]
The suitors then embarked and sailed away
on their trip across the water, minds fully bent
on slaughtering Telemachus. Out at sea,
half way between Ithaca and rugged Samos,
there's the rocky island Asteris. It's small,
but ships can moor there in a place with openings
in both directions. The Achaeans waited there   40
and set up their ambush for Telemachus.

BOOK FIVE

V

ODYSSEUS LEAVES CALYPSO AND REACHES PHAEACIA

As Dawn stirred from her bed beside lord Tithonus,
bringing light to eternal gods and mortal men,
the gods were sitting in assembly, among them
high-thundering Zeus, whose power is supreme.
Athena was reminding them of all the stories
of Odysseus' troubles—she was concerned for him
as he passed his days in nymph Calypso's home.

> "Father Zeus and you other blessed gods
> who live forever, let no sceptred king
> be prudent, kind, or gentle from now on,   10
> or think about his fate. Let him instead
> always be cruel and treat men viciously,   [10]
> since no one now has any memory
> of lord Odysseus, who ruled his people
> and was a gentle father. Now he lies
> suffering extreme distress on that island
> where nymph Calypso lives. She keeps him there
> by force, and he's unable to sail off.
> And now some men are setting out to kill
> the son he loves, as he sails home. The boy   20
> has gone to gather news about his father,
> off to sacred Pylos and holy Sparta."   [20]

Cloud-gatherer Zeus then answered her and said:

>   "My child,
> did you not organize this plan yourself,
> so that Odysseus, once he made it home,
> could take out his revenge against those men?
> As for Telemachus, you should use your skill
> to get him to his native land unharmed—
> that's well within your power. The suitors
> will sail back in their ship without success."   30

Zeus spoke and then instructed Hermes, his dear son:

> "Hermes, tell the fair-haired nymph   [30]
> my firm decision—the brave Odysseus
> is to get back home. He'll get no guidance
> from the gods or mortal men, but sail off
> on a raft of wood well lashed together."

22

Zeus finished speaking. The killer of Argus,
his messenger, obeyed. At once he laced up
on his feet those lovely golden ageless sandals
which carry him as fast as stormy blasts of wind.   40
When he reached the distant island, he rose up,
out of the violet sea, and moved on shore,
until he reached the massive cave, where Calypso,
the fair-haired nymph, had her home. He found her there,
a huge fire blazing in her hearth—from far away
the smell of split cedar and burning sandal wood   [60]
spread across the island. With her lovely voice
Calypso sang inside the cave, as she moved
back and forth before her loom—she was weaving
with a golden shuttle. All around her cave   50
trees were in bloom, alder and sweet-smelling cypress,
and poplar, too, with long-winged birds nesting there—
owls, hawks, and chattering sea crows, who spend their time
out on the water. A garden vine, fully ripe
and rich with grapes, trailed through the hollow cave.
From four fountains, close to each other in a row,   [70]
clear water flowed in various directions,
and all around soft meadows spread out in full bloom
with violets and parsley. Even a god,
who lives forever, coming there, would be amazed   60
to see it, and his heart would fill with pleasure.
The killer of Argus, god's messenger, stood there,
marvelling at the sight. But once his spirit
had contemplated all these things with wonder,
he went inside the spacious cave. And Calypso,
that lovely goddess, when she saw him face to face,
was not ignorant of who he was, for the gods
are not unknown to one another, even though
the home of some immortal might be far away.   [80]
But Hermes did not find Odysseus in the cave—   70
that great-hearted man sat crying on the shore,
just as before, breaking his heart with tears and groans,
full of sorrow, as he looked out on the restless sea
and wept. Calypso invited Hermes to sit down
on a bright shining chair. Then the lovely goddess
questioned him:

   "Hermes, honoured and welcome guest,
why have you come here with your golden wand?
You haven't been a visitor before.

Tell me what's on your mind. My heart desires
to carry out what you request, if I can,   80
and if it's something fated to be done."   [90]

After this speech, Calypso set out a table
laden with ambrosia, then mixed red nectar.
And so the messenger god, killer of Argus,
ate and drank. When his meal was over and the food
had comforted his heart, Hermes gave his answer,
speaking to Calypso with these words:

                    "You're a goddess,
Since you've questioned me, I'll tell you the truth.
Zeus told me to come here against my will.
He says that you have here with you a man   90
more unfortunate than all the other ones
who fought nine years round Priam's city,
which in the tenth year they destroyed and left
to get back home. Now Zeus is ordering you
to send him off as soon as possible."

The killer of Argus, the gods' great messenger,
said these words and left. The regal nymph Calypso,
once she'd heard Zeus' message, went off to find   [150]
great-hearted Odysseus. She found him by the shore,
sitting down, with his eyes always full of tears,   100
because his sweet life was passing while he mourned
for his return. The nymph no longer gave him joy.
At night he slept beside her in the hollow cave,
as he was forced to do—not of his own free will,
though she was eager enough. Moving up,
close to him, the lovely goddess spoke:

                    "Poor man,   [160]
spend no more time in sorrow on this island
or waste your life away. My heart agrees—
the time has come for me to send you off.
So come now, cut long timbers with an axe,   110
and make a raft, a large one. Build a deck
high up on it, so it can carry you
across the misty sea. I'll provision it
with as much food and water and red wine
as you will need to satisfy your wants."   [170]

As soon as rose-fingered early Dawn appeared,
Odysseus quickly put on a cloak and tunic,

and the nymph dressed in a long white shining robe,   [230]
a lovely woven dress. Then she organized her plans
so brave Odysseus could leave. She handed him   120
a massive axe, well suited to his grip, and made
of two-edged bronze. It had a finely crafted shaft
of handsome olive wood. Next she provided him
a polished adze. Then she led him on a path
down to the edges of the island, where tall trees grew,
alder, poplar, and pine that reached the upper sky,
well-seasoned, dried-out wood, which could keep him afloat.   [240]
Once she'd pointed out to him where the large trees grew,
Calypso, the lovely goddess, went back home.
Odysseus then began to cut the timber. His work   130
proceeded quickly. He cut down twenty trees,
used his bronze axe to trim and deftly smooth them,
then lined them up. The fair goddess Calypso
then brought him augers, so he bored each timber,
fastened them to one another, and tightened them
with pins and binding. Next he set up a mast
with a yard arm fastened to it and then made
a steering oar to guide the raft. Calypso,
the beautiful goddess, brought him woven cloth
to make a sail—which he did very skillfully.   140
On it he tied bracing ropes, sheets, and halyards,   [260]
and then levered the raft down to the shining sea.

By the fourth day he had completed all this work.
So on the fifth beautiful Calypso bathed him,
dressed him in sweet-smelling clothes, and sent him
from the island. The goddess stowed on board the raft
a sack full of dark wine and another large one,
full of water, and a bag of food, in which she put
many tasty things for him to eat. She sent him
a warm and gentle wind, and lord Odysseus sailed   150
for ten days on the water, then for seven more,
and on the eighteenth day some shadowy hills appeared,
where the land of the Phaeacians, like a shield   [280]
riding on the misty sea, lay very close to him.

Poseidon watched Odysseus sailing on the sea,
and his spirit grew enraged. He shook his head
and spoke to his own heart:

                              "Something's wrong!
The gods must have changed what they were planning

25

for Odysseus, while I've been far away
among the Ethiopians. For now   160
he's hard by the land of the Phaeacians,
where he'll escape the great extremes of sorrow
which have come over him—so Fate ordains.
But still, even now I think I'll push him   [290]
so he gets his fill of troubles."

                                         Poseidon spoke.
Then he drove the clouds together, seized his trident,
and shook up the sea. He brought on stormy blasts
from every kind of wind, concealing land and sea
with clouds, so darkness fell from heaven. East Wind
clashed with South Wind, while West Wind, raging in a storm,   170
smashed into North Wind, born in the upper sky,
as it pushed a massive wave. Odysseus' knees gave way,
his spirit fell, and in great distress he spoke aloud,
addressing his great heart:

                    "I've got such a wretched fate!
How is all this going to end up for me?   [300]
I'm afraid everything the goddess said
was true, when she claimed that out at sea,
before I got back to my native land,
I'd have my fill of troubles."

                                     As he said this,
a massive wave charged at him with tremendous force,   180
swirled round the raft, then from high above crashed down.
Odysseus let go his grip on the steering oar
and fell out, a long way from the raft. The fierce gusts
of howling winds snapped the mast off in the middle.
Then Athena, Zeus' daughter, thought up something new.
She blocked the paths of every wind but one
and ordered all of them to stop and check their force,
then roused the swift North Wind and broke the waves in front,
so divinely born Odysseus might yet meet
the people of Phaeacia, who love the oar,   190
avoiding death and Fates.[1]

---

[1]The phrase "divinely born" and other similar phrases which are sometimes applied
to Odysseus are marks of his nobility. They are not to be taken literally. Odysseus
is the son of a mortal, Laertes. Laertes' father, Arcesius, was a son of Zeus.

BOOK FIVE

So for two days and nights
he floated on the ocean waves, his heart filled
with many thoughts of death. But when fair-haired Dawn   [390]
gave rise at last to the third day, the wind died down,
the sea grew calm and still. He was lifted up
by a large swell, and as he quickly looked ahead,
Odysseus saw land close by. He kept swimming on
and reached the mouth of a fair-flowing river,
which seemed to him the finest place to go onshore.
There were no rocks, and it was sheltered from the wind.   200
Odysseus recognized the river as it flowed
and prayed to him deep in his heart. At once the god
held back his flow, checked the waves, calmed the water,
and brought him safely to the river mouth. Both knees bent,
he let his strong hands fall—the sea had crushed his spirit.
All his skin was swollen, sea water flowed in streams
up in his mouth and nose. He lay there breathless,
without a word, hardly moving—quite overcome
with terrible exhaustion. Then by the water
he found a place with a wide view. So he crept   210
underneath two bushes growing from one stem—
one was an olive tree, the other a wild thorn.
Athena then poured sleep onto his eyes,
covering his eyelids, so he could find relief,
a quick respite from his exhausting troubles.

Book Six

VI

Odysseus and Nausicaa

While much-enduring lord Odysseus slept there,
overcome with weariness and sleep, Athena
went to the land of the Phaeacians, to their city,
to arrange a journey home for brave Odysseus.
She moved into a wonderfully furnished room
where a young girl slept, one like immortal goddesses
in form and loveliness. She was Nausicaa,
daughter of great-hearted Alcinous. Like a gust of wind,   [20]
Athena slipped over to the young girl's bedside,
stood there above her head, and then spoke to her.   10
Her appearance changed to look like Dymas' daughter—
a young girl the same age as Nausicaa,
whose heart was well disposed to her. In that form,
bright-eyed Athena spoke out and said:

                         "Nausicaa,
how did your mother bear a girl so careless?   [30]
Your splendid clothes are lying here uncared for.
And your wedding day is not so far away,
when you must dress up in expensive robes
and give them to your wedding escort, too.
You know it's things like these that help to make   20
a noble reputation among men
and please your honoured mother and father.
Come, at daybreak let's wash out the clothing.
Ask your noble father to provide you,
this morning early, a wagon and some mules,
so you can carry the bright coverlets,
the robes and sashes. That would be better
than going on foot, because the washing tubs
are located some distance from the town."   [40]

As soon as Dawn on her splendid throne arrived   30
and woke fair-robed Nausicaa, she was curious
about her dream. So she moved through the house.   [50]
Nausicaa went to stand close by her father
and then spoke to him:

                    "Dear father, can you prepare
a high wagon with sturdy wheels for me,
so I can carry my fine clothing out
and wash it in the river? It's lying here

28

all dirty. And it's appropriate for you
to wear fresh garments on your person
when you're with our leading men in council.   40
You have five dear sons living in your home—
two are married, but three are now young men
still unattached, and they always require
fresh-washed clothing when they go out dancing.
All these things I have to think about."

Nausicaa said these words because she felt ashamed
to remind her father of her own happy thoughts
of getting married. But he understood all that
and answered, saying:

        "I have no objection,
my child, to providing mules for you,   50
or any other things. Go on your way.
Slaves will get a four-wheeled wagon ready
with a high box framed on top."   [70]

        Once he'd said this,
he called out to his slaves, and they did what he ordered.
They prepared a smooth-running wagon made for mules,
led up the animals, and then yoked them to it.
Nausicaa brought her fine clothing from her room.
She placed it in the polished wagon bed. Her mother
loaded on a box full of all sorts of tasty food.
She put in delicacies, as well, and poured some wine   60
into a goat skin. The girl climbed on the wagon.
With a clatter of hooves, the mules moved quickly off,
carrying the clothing and the girl, not by herself,
for her attendants went with her as well.

When they reached the stream of the fair-flowing river,
the girls picked up the clothing from the wagon,
carried it in their arms down to the murky water,
and trampled it inside the washing trenches,
each one trying to work more quickly than the others.
Once they'd washed the clothes and cleaned off all the stains,   70
they laid the garments out in rows along the sea shore,
right where the waves which beat upon the coast
had washed the pebbles clean. Once they had bathed themselves
and rubbed their bodies well with oil, they ate a meal
beside the river mouth, waiting for the clothes to dry
in the sun's warm rays. When they'd enjoyed their food,

the girl and her attendants threw their head scarves off   [100]
to play catch with a ball, and white-armed Nausicaa
led them in song. But when the princess threw the ball
at one of those attendants with her, she missed the girl   80
and tossed it in the deep and swirling river.
They gave a piercing cry which woke up lord Odysseus.
So he sat up, thinking in his heart and mind:

    "Here's trouble! In this country I have reached,
    what are the people like? Are they violent
    and wild, without a sense of justice?   [120]
    Or are they kind to strangers? In their minds
    do they fear the gods? A young woman's shout
    rang out around me—nymphs who live along
    steep mountain peaks and by the river springs   90
    and grassy meadows. Could I somehow be
    near men with human speech? Come on then,
    I'm going to try to find out for myself."

With these words, lord Odysseus crept out from the thicket.
With his strong hands, he broke off from thick bushes
a leafy branch to hold across his body and conceal
his sexual organs. He emerged, moving just like
a mountain lion which relies on its own strength—   [130]
though hammered by the rain and wind, it creeps ahead,
its two eyes burning, coming in among the herd   100
of sheep or cattle, or stalking a wild deer—
his belly tells him to move in against the flocks,
even within a well-built farm. That's how Odysseus
was coming out to meet those fair-haired girls,
although he was stark naked. He was in great distress,
but, caked with brine, he was a fearful sight to them,
and they ran off in fear and crouched down here and there
among the jutting dunes of sand. The only one
to stand her ground was Alcinous' daughter.
So he quickly used his cunning and spoke to her   110
with soothing language:

            "O divine queen,
    I come here as a suppliant to you.
    Are you a goddess or a mortal being?
    If you're one of the gods who hold wide heaven,   [150]
    then I think you most resemble Artemis,
    daughter of great Zeus, in your loveliness,
    your stature, and your shape. If you're human,

one of those mortals living on the earth,
your father and noble mother are thrice-blest,
and thrice-blest your brothers, too. In their hearts   120
they must glow with pleasure for you always,
when they see a child like you moving up
into the dance. But the happiest heart,
more so than all the rest, belongs to him
who with his wedding gifts will lead you home.
But great distress has overtaken me.
Yesterday, my twentieth day afloat,
I escaped the wine-dark sea. Before that,
waves and swift-driving storm winds carried me
from Ogygia island. And now a god   130
has tossed me on shore here, so that somehow
I'll suffer trouble in this place as well.
For I don't think my problems will end now.
Before that day, there are still many more
the gods will bring about. But, divine queen,
have pity. You're the first one I've approached,
after going through so much grief. I don't know
any other people, none of those who hold
the city and its land. Show me the town.
Give me some rag to throw around myself,   140
perhaps some wrapping you had for the clothes."

White-armed Nausicaa then answered him and said:

"Stranger, you don't seem to be a wicked man,
or foolish. Olympian Zeus himself
gives happiness to bad and worthy men,
each one receiving just what Zeus desires.
But now you've reached our land and city,
you'll not lack clothes or any other thing
we owe a hard-pressed suppliant we meet.
I'll show the town to you, and I'll tell you   150
what our country's called—the Phaeacians
own this city and this land. As for me,
I am the daughter of brave Alcinous—
Phaeacian power and strength depend on him."

Nausicaa finished speaking. Then she called out
to her fair-haired attendants:

                    "Stand up, you girls,
Have you run off because you've seen a man?

31

Surely you don't think he's an enemy?   [200]
So, my girls, give this stranger food and drink.
Then bathe him in the river, in a place   160
where there's some shelter from the wind."   [210]

Nausicaa finished. They stood up and called out
to one another. Then they took Odysseus aside,
to a sheltered spot, following what Nausicaa,
daughter of great-hearted Alcinous, had ordered.
They set out clothing for him, a cloak and tunic,
and gave him the gold flask full of smooth olive oil.
They told him to bathe there in the flowing river.

When he'd washed himself all over and rubbed on oil,   170
he put on clothes the unmarried girl had given him.
Then Odysseus went to sit some distance off,
beside the shore, glowing with charm and beauty.
Nausicaa gazed at him in admiration. They set out
food and drink before resourceful lord Odysseus.
He ate and drank voraciously—many days had passed   [250]
since he'd last tasted food. Then white-armed Nausicaa
thought of something else. She folded up the clothes,
put them in the handsome wagon, harnessed up
the strong-hooved mules, and climbed up by herself.   180
She called out to Odysseus then spoke to him:

"Get up now, stranger, and go to the city.
I'll take you to my wise father's house,
where, I tell you, you will get to meet
all the finest of Phaeacians. You seem
to me to have good sense, so act as follows—
while we are moving through the countryside
past men's farms, walk fast with my attendants   [260]
behind the mules and wagon. I'll lead the way.
You'll come across a fine grove to Athena—   190
it's near the road, a clump of poplar trees.
There's a fountain, with meadows all around.
My father has a fertile vineyard there,
some land, as well, within shouting distance
of the town. Sit down there, and wait a while,
until we move into the city and reach
my father's house. When you think we've had time
to reach my home, then go in the city
of the Phaeacians and inquire about
my father's house, great-hearted Alcinous.   200

Once inside the house and in the courtyard,
move through the great hall quickly till you reach
my mother seated at the hearth, in the firelight,
against a pillar, spinning purple yarn—
a marvellous sight. Servants sit behind her.
If her heart and mind are well-disposed to you,
then there is hope you'll see your friends and reach
your well-built house and your own native land."

Saying this, Nausicaa cracked the shining whip
and struck the mules. They quickly left the flowing river,   210
moving briskly forward at a rapid pace.
Using her judgment with the whip, she drove on   [320]
so Odysseus and her servants could keep up on foot.
Just at sunset, they reached the celebrated grove,
sacred to Athena. Lord Odysseus sat down there
and made a quick prayer to great Zeus' daughter.

33

VII

ODYSSEUS AT THE COURT OF ALCINOUS IN PHAEACIA

So lord Odysseus, who had endured so much, prayed there,
while two strong mules took the girl into the city.
Then Odysseus got up and set off for the palace.
The Phaeacians, so celebrated for their ships,
did not see him as he moved across the city
in their midst. Athena, fair-haired fearful goddess,   [40]
would not permit that. Her heart cared about him,
so she cast around him an amazing mist.

*[Athena disguised as a young girl meets Odysseus and tells him
about the royal family of Phaeacia and instructs him how to behave
when he gets to the royal court.]*

Odysseus moved towards Alcinous' splendid home.
Above the high-vaulted home of brave Alcinous   10
there was a radiance, as if from sun or moon.
Bronze walls extended out beyond the threshold
in various directions to the inner rooms,
which had a blue enamel cornice. Golden doors
blocked the way into the well-constructed palace.
The bronze threshold had silver doorposts set inside
and a silver lintel. The handles were of gold.   [90]
On both sides of the door stood gold and silver dogs,
immortal creatures who would never age,
created by Hephaestus' matchless artistry,   20
to guard the palace of great-hearted Alcinous.[1]
Lord Odysseus, who had endured so much, stood there
and gazed around. When his heart had marvelled at it all,
he moved fast across the threshold into the house.
Long-suffering lord Odysseus, still enclosed in mist,
the thick covering poured around him by Athena,   [140]
went through the hall until he came to Arete
and Alcinous, the king. With his arms Odysseus
embraced the knees of Arete, and at that moment
the miraculous mist dissolved away from him.   30
The people in the palace were all silent,
as they gazed upon the man, struck with wonder
at the sight. Odysseus then made this entreaty:

---

[1]Hephaestus, one of the Olympian gods, son of Zeus and Hera, is the craftsman-
creator god of the forge.

"Arete, daughter of godlike Rhexenor,
I've come to you and to your husband here,
to your knees, in supplication to you—
a man who's experienced so much distress—
and to those feasting here. May gods grant them
happiness in life, and may they each pass on
riches in their homes to all their children,   40   [150]
and noble honours given by the people.
Please rouse yourself to help me return home,
to get back quickly to my native land.
I've been suffering trouble for a long time
so far away from friends."

            When he heard these words,
brave and kingly Alcinous stretched out his hand,
reached for Odysseus, that wise and crafty man,
raised him from the hearth, and invited him to sit.
Then royal Alcinous spoke to his herald:

"Pontonous, prepare wine in the mixing bowl,   50
then serve it to all people in the hall,
so we may pour libations out to Zeus,   [180]
who loves lightning, for he accompanies
all pious suppliants."

            Once Alcinous said this,
Pontonous prepared the honeyed wine, and then poured
the first drops for libation into every cup.
When they'd made their offering and drunk their fill of wine,
Alcinous then addressed the gathering and said:

"You Phaeacian counsellors and leaders,
pay attention to me so I can say   60
what the heart here in my chest commands.
Now that you have all finished eating,
return back to your homes and get some rest.
In the morning we'll summon an assembly
with more elders, entertain this stranger   [190]
here in our home, and also sacrifice
choice offerings to the gods. Then after that,
we'll think about how we can send him off,
so that this stranger, with us escorting him
and without further pain or effort, may reach   70
his native land, no matter how far distant.
Meanwhile he'll not suffer harm or trouble,

35

not before he sets foot on his own land.
After that he'll undergo all those things
Destiny and the dreaded spinning Fates
spun in the thread for him when he was born,
when his mother gave him birth.[1] However,
if he's a deathless one come down from heaven,
then gods are planning something different."   [200]

Resourceful Odysseus then answered Alcinous: 80

"Alcinous, you should not concern yourself
about what you've just said—for I'm not like
the immortal gods who hold wide heaven,
not in my form or shape. I'm like mortal men.   [210]
Indeed, I could recount a longer story—
all those hardships I have had to suffer
from the gods. But let me eat my dinner,
though I'm in great distress. For there's nothing
more shameless than a wretched stomach,
which commands a man to think about its needs,   90
even if he's really sad or troubles
weigh down his heart, just the way my spirit
is now full of sorrow, yet my belly
is always telling me to eat and drink,   [220]
forgetting everything I've had to bear,
and ordering me to stuff myself with food.
But when Dawn appears, you should stir yourselves
so you can set me in my misery
back on my native soil, for all I've suffered.
If I can see my goods again, my slaves,   100
my large and high-roofed home, then let life end."

Once Odysseus finished, they all approved his words,
and, because he'd spoken well and to the point,
they ordered that their guest should be sent on his way.

*[Odysseus tells Alcinous and Arete the story of his voyage from
Calypso's island to Phaeacia and of his treatment by Nausicaa.
Then they all retire to bed for the night.]*

---

[1]The three Fates, who are sisters, are called Atropos, Lachesis, and Clotho. At a
person's birth they allot his or her share of pain and suffering and good. According
to some accounts, Clotho sets the wool around the spindle, Lachesis spins the
yarn, and Atropos cuts the thread when death comes. The Olympian gods cannot
or will not alter the decisions of the Fates.

BOOK EIGHT

VIII

ODYSSEUS IS ENTERTAINED IN PHAEACIA

The next day king Alcinous addressed them all
and said to the Phaeacians:

> "Listen to me,
> you Phaeacian counsellors and leaders.
> I'll tell you what the heart in my chest says.
> This stranger here, a man I do not know,
> a wanderer, has travelled to my house.
> He's asking to be sent away back home   [30]
> and has requested confirmation from us.
> So let us act as we have done before
> and assist him with his journey. No man   10
> arriving at my palace stays there long
> grieving because he cannot get back home."

Alcinous spoke and led them off. The sceptred kings
came after him, while a herald went to find
the godlike singer. Fifty-two hand-picked young men
went off, as Alcinous had ordered, to the shore
beside the restless sea. Once they reached the boat,   [50]
they dragged the black ship into deeper water,
set the mast and sails in place inside the vessel,
lashed the rowing oars onto their leather pivots,   20
then hoisted the white sail. Next, they moored the ship
well out to sea and then returned to the great home
of their wise king. Halls, corridors, and courtyards
were full of people gathering—a massive crowd,
young and old. On their behalf Alcinous slaughtered
eight white-tusked boars, two shambling oxen, and twelve sheep.   [60]
These carcasses they skinned and dressed and then prepared
a splendid banquet. Meanwhile the herald was returning
with the loyal singer, a man the Muse so loved
above all others. She'd given him both bad and good,   30
for she'd destroyed his eyes, but had bestowed on him
the gift of pleasing song. The herald, Pontonous,
then brought up a silver-studded chair for him.
Once they'd enjoyed their heart's fill of food and drink,
the minstrel was inspired by the Muse to sing
a song about the glorious deeds of warriors,
that tale, whose fame had climbed to spacious heaven,
about Odysseus and Achilles, son of Peleus,

when, at a lavish feast in honour of the gods,
they'd fought each other in ferocious argument.[1]   40
This was the song the celebrated minstrel sang.

Alcinous then asked Laodamas and Halius   [370]
to dance alone. No man could match their dancing skill.
The two men picked up a lovely purple ball,
Then, leaning back, one of them would throw it high,
towards the shadowy clouds, and then the other,
before his feet touched ground, would catch it easily.
Once they had shown their skill in tossing it straight up,
they threw it back and forth, as they kept dancing
on the life-sustaining earth, while more young men   50
stood at the edge of the arena, beating time.
The dancing rhythms made a powerful sound.   [380]
Then lord Odysseus spoke:

> "Mighty Alcinous,
most renowned among all men, you claimed
your dancers were the best, and now, indeed,
what you said is true. When I gaze at them,
I'm lost in wonder."

At Odysseus' words,
powerful king Alcinous felt a great delight,
and spoke at once to his Phaeacians, master sailors.

"Leaders and counsellors of the Phaeacians,   60
listen—this stranger seems to me a man
with an uncommon wisdom. So come now,
let's give him gifts of friendship, as is right.
Twelve distinguished kings are rulers here   [390]
and govern in this land, and I myself
am the thirteenth king. Let each of you
bring a fresh cloak and tunic, newly washed,
and a talent of pure gold. All of this
we should put together very quickly,
so this stranger has his gifts in hand   70
and goes to dinner with a joyful heart."

Alcinous spoke. All those present agreed with him
and said it should be done. Then every one of them
sent an attendant out to bring back presents.

---

[1]These lines refer to an argument between Odysseus and Achilles about the best
tactics to use against the Trojans.

As the sun went down, splendid presents were brought in,
carried to Alcinous' home by worthy heralds.
The sons of noble Alcinous took the lovely gifts   [420]
and set them down before their honoured mother.
Nausicaa, whose beauty was a gift from god,
standing by the doorway of that well-built hall,   80
looked at Odysseus and was filled with wonder.
She spoke winged words to him: [460]

> "Farewell, stranger.
When you are back in your own land,
I hope you will remember me sometimes,
since you owe your life to me."

     Then Odysseus,
that resourceful man, replied to her and said:

> "Nausicaa, daughter of great Alcinous,
may Hera's loud-thundering husband, Zeus,
grant that I see the day of my return
when I get home. There I will pray to you   90
all my days, as to a god. For you, girl,
you gave me my life."

     Odysseus finished speaking.
Then he sat down on a chair beside king Alcinous.
who spoke out at once, addressing his Phaeacians,
lovers of the sea.

>   "Listen to me,
you Phaeacians counsellors and leaders.
To any man with some intelligence,
a stranger coming as a suppliant
brings the same delight a brother does.
And you, our guest, should no longer hide   100
behind those cunning thoughts of yours and skirt
the things I ask you. It's better to be frank.
Tell me your name, what they call you at home—   [550]
your mother and your father and the others,
those in the town and in the countryside.
Tell me your country and your people,
your city, too, so ships can take you there,
using what they know to chart their passage."

BOOK NINE

IX

ISMARUS, THE LOTUS EATERS, AND THE CYCLOPS

Resourceful Odysseus then replied to Alcinous:

"Lord Alcinous, most renowned of men,
there's nothing gives one more delight
than when joy grips entire groups of men
who sit in proper order in a hall
feasting and listening to a singer,
with tables standing there beside them
laden with bread and meat, as the steward
draws wine out of the mixing bowl, moves round,   [10]
and fills the cups. To my mind this seems   10
the finest thing there is. But your heart
wants to ask about my grievous sorrows,
so I can weep and groan more than before.
What shall I tell you first? Where do I stop?
For the heavenly gods have given me
so much distress. Well, I will make a start
by telling you my name. Once you know that,
if I escape the painful day of death,
then later I can welcome you as guests,
though I live in a palace far away.   20
I am Odysseus, son of Laertes,
well known to all for my deceptive skills—
my fame extends all the way to heaven.   [20]
I live in Ithaca, a land of sunshine.
From far away one sees a mountain there,
thick with whispering trees, Mount Neriton,
and many islands lying around it
close together. It's a rugged island,
but nurtures fine young men. Come, I'll tell you
of the miserable journey back which Zeus   30
arranged for me when I returned from Troy.[1]

"I was carried by the wind from Troy
to Ismarus, land of the Cicones.
I destroyed the city there, killed the men,   [40]
seized their wives, and captured lots of treasure

---

[1]For a chart of the various adventures of Odysseus on his way home, consult the
map at the end of this book (p. 171). His first adventure, at Ismarus with the
Cicones, seems to have been on the mainland north of Troy.

which we divided up. I took great pains
to see that all men got an equal share.
Then I gave orders we should leave on foot—
and with all speed. But the men were fools.
They didn't listen. They drank too much wine   40
and on the shoreline slaughtered many sheep,
as well as shambling cows with twisted horns.
Meanwhile the Cicones set off and gathered up
their neighbours, tribesmen living further inland.
They reached us in the morning, thick as leaves
or flowers growing in season. Then Zeus
brought us disaster—he made that our fate,
so we would suffer many casualties.
They set their ranks and fought by our swift ships.
We threw our bronze-tipped spears at one another.   50
While morning lasted and that sacred day
gained strength, we held our ground and beat them back,
for all their greater numbers. But as the sun
moved to the hour when oxen are unyoked,
the Cicones broke through, overpowering
Achaeans. Of my well-armed companions,   [60]
six from every ship were killed. The rest of us
made our escape, avoiding Death and Fate.

"We sailed away from there, hearts full of grief
at losing loyal companions, though happy   60
we'd eluded death ourselves. Cloud-gatherer Zeus
then stirred North Wind to rage against our ships—
a violent storm concealing land and sea,
Nine days fierce winds drove me away from there,
across the fish-filled seas, and on the tenth
we landed where the Lotus-eaters live,
people who feed upon its flowering fruit.[1]
We went ashore and carried water back.
Then my companions quickly had a meal
by our swift ships. We had our food and drink,   70
and then I sent some of my comrades out
to learn about the men who ate the food
the land grew there. I chose two of my men   [90]
and with them sent a third as messenger.
They left at once and met the Lotus-eaters,

[1]The land of the Lotus Eaters is commonly placed in North Africa.

who had no thought of killing my companions,
but gave them lotus plants to eat, whose fruit,
sweet as honey, made any man who tried it
lose his desire ever to journey home
or bring back word to us—they wished to stay,   80
to remain among the Lotus-eaters,
feeding on the plant, eager to forget
about their homeward voyage. I forced them,
eyes full of tears, into our hollow ships,
dragged them underneath the rowing benches,
and tied them up. Then I issued orders   [100]
for my other trusty comrades to embark
and sail away with speed in our fast ships,
in case another man might eat a lotus
and lose all thoughts about his journey back.   90

"We sailed away from there with heavy hearts
and reached the country of the Cyclopes,
a crude and lawless people.[1] They don't grow
any plants by hand or plough the earth,
but put their trust in the immortal gods,
and though they never sow or work the land,
every kind of crop springs up for them—
wheat and barley and rich grape-bearing vines,   [110]
and Zeus provides the rain to make them grow.
They live without a council or assembly   100
or any rule of law, in hollow caves
among the mountain tops. Each one of them
makes laws for his own wives and children,
and they shun all dealings with each other.

"Now, near the country of the Cyclopes,
outside the harbour, there's a fertile island,
covered in trees, some distance from the shore,
but not too far away. Wild goats live there
in countless numbers. They have no need

---

[1]The Cyclopes (singular Cyclops) are hairy monsters, rather than people, with only one eye in the middle of their foreheads. They originated from the primal gods, Ouranos and Gaia, and had been imprisoned in Tartarus. But they helped Zeus in his fight against his father, Cronos, and Zeus freed them. Odysseus, one assumes, either doesn't know about the Cyclopes before this adventure or is not aware he is about to meet one, since he assumes he is moving into a place where the laws of hospitality apply. Most geographical interpretations place the incident with the cyclops in Sicily. We learn later that the cyclops Odysseus meets has a name (Polyphemus) and is, along with his neighbours, a son of Poseidon.

to stay away from any human trails.   110
At the harbour head there is a water spring—   [140]
a bright stream flows out underneath a cave.
Around it poplars grow. We sailed in there.
Some god led us in through the murky night—
we couldn't see a thing, and all our ships
were swallowed up in fog. Clouds hid the moon,
so there was no light coming from the sky.
Our eyes could not catch any glimpse of land
or of the long waves rolling in onshore,
until our well-decked ships had reached the beach.   120
We hauled up our ships, took down all the sails,
went up along the shore, and fell asleep,   [150]
remaining there until the light of Dawn.

"As soon as rose-fingered early Dawn appeared,   [170]
I called a meeting and spoke to all the men:

    'My loyal comrades, stay here where you are.
I'll take my ship and my own company
and try to find out who those people are,
whether they are rough and violent,
with no sense of law, or kind to strangers,   130
with hearts that fear the gods.'

        "I said these words,
then went down to my ship and told my crew
to loose the cables lashed onto the stern
and come onboard. They embarked with speed,
and, seated at the oarlocks in their rows,
struck the grey sea with their oars. And then,   [180]
when we'd made the short trip round the island,
on the coast there, right beside the sea,
we saw a high cave, overhung with laurel.
There were many flocks, sheep as well as goats,   140
penned in there at night. All around the cave
there was a high front courtyard made of stones
set deep into the ground, with tall pine trees
and towering oaks. At night a giant slept there,
one that grazed his flocks all by himself,
somewhere far off. He avoided others
and lived alone, away from all the rest,
a law unto himself, a monster, made   [190]
to be a thing of wonder, not like man
who lives by eating bread, no, more like   150

43

a lofty wooded mountain crag, standing there
to view in isolation from the rest.

"I told the rest of my trustworthy crew
to stay there by the ship and guard it,
while I selected twelve of my best men
and went off to explore. I took with me
a goatskin full of dark sweet wine. Maron,
Euanthes' son, one of Apollo's priests,
the god who kept guard over Ismarus,
gave it to me because, to show respect,   160
we had protected him, his wife, and child.
Each time they drank that honey-sweet red wine,
he'd fill one cup with it and pour that out
in twenty cups of water, and the smell
arising from the mixing bowl was sweet,   [210]
astonishingly so—to tell the truth,
no one's heart could then refuse to drink it.

"We soon reached his cave but didn't find him.
He was pasturing his rich flocks in the fields.
We went inside the cave and looked around.   170
It was astonishing—crates full of cheese,
pens crammed with livestock—lambs and kids
sorted into separate groups, with yearlings,   [220]
older lambs, and newborns each in different pens.
All the sturdy buckets, pails, and milking bowls
were awash with whey. At first, my comrades
urged me to grab some cheeses and return,
then drive the lambs and kids out of their pens
back to our swift ship and cross the water.
But I did not agree, though if I had,   180
things would have been much better. I was keen
to see the man in person and find out
if he would show me hospitality."

"We lit a fire and offered sacrifice.
Then we helped ourselves to cheese and ate it.
We stayed inside the cave and waited there,
until he led his flocks back home. He came,
bearing an enormous pile of dried-out wood
to cook his dinner. He hurled his load
inside the cave with a huge crash. In our fear,   190
we moved back to the far end of the cave,
into the deepest corner. He then drove

44

his fat flock right inside the spacious cavern,
just the ones he milked. Rams and billy goats
he left outside, in the open courtyard.
Then he raised up high a massive boulder   [240]
and fixed it in position as a door.
It was huge—twenty-two four-wheeled wagons,
good ones, too, could not have shifted it
along the ground—that's how immense it was,   200
the rock he planted right in his doorway.
He sat down with his bleating goats and ewes
and milked them all, each in turn, setting
beside each one its young. Next, he curdled
half the white milk and set aside the whey
in wicker baskets, then put the other half
in bowls for him to drink up with his dinner.
Once he'd finished working at these tasks,   [250]
he lit a fire. Then he spied us and said:

                                        'Strangers,
who are you? What sea route brought you here?   210
Are you trading men, or wandering the sea
at random, like pirates sailing anywhere,
risking their lives to injure other men.'

"As he spoke, our hearts collapsed, terrified
by his deep voice and monstrous size. But still,
I answered him by saying:

                                        'We are Achaeans
coming back from Troy and blown off course
by various winds across vast tracts of sea.   [260]
So, good sir, respect the gods. We're here
as suppliants to you, and Zeus protects   220 [270]
all suppliants and strangers—as god of guests,
he cares for all respected visitors.'

"I finished speaking. He answered me at once—
his heart was pitiless:

                                'What fools you are,
you strangers, or else you come from far away—
telling me to fear the gods and shun their rage.
The Cyclopes care nothing about Zeus,
who bears the aegis, or the blessed gods.
We are much more powerful than them.
I wouldn't spare you or your comrades   230

to escape the wrath of Zeus, not unless
my own heart prompted me to do it.
But now, tell me this—when you landed here,
where did you moor your ship, a spot close by
or further off? I'd like to know that.'   [280]

"He said this to throw me off, but his deceit
could never fool me. I was too clever.
And so I gave him a cunning answer:

    'Earthshaker Poseidon broke my ship apart—
    driving it against the border of your island,   240
    on the rocks there. He brought us close to land,
    hard by the headland, then winds pushed us
    inshore from the sea. But we escaped—
    me and these men here. We weren't destroyed.'

"That's what I said. But his ruthless heart
gave me no reply. Instead, he jumped up,
seized two of my companions in his fist,
and smashed them on the ground like puppy dogs.
Their brains oozed out and soaked the ground below.   [290]
He tore their limbs apart to make a meal,   250
and chewed them up just like a mountain lion—
innards, flesh, and marrow—leaving nothing.
We raised our hands to Zeus and cried aloud,
to witness the horrific things he did,
our hearts unable to do anything.
Once Cyclops had stuffed his massive stomach
with human flesh and washed it down with milk,
he lay down in the cave, stretched out there
among his flocks. Then, in my courageous heart
I formed a plan to move up close beside him,   260
draw the sharp sword I carried on my thigh,   [300]
and run my hand along his chest, to find
exactly where his midriff held his liver,
then stick him there. But I had second thoughts.
We, too, would have been utterly destroyed,
there in the cave—we didn't have the strength
with our own hands to roll from the high door
the massive rock he'd set there. So we groaned,
and stayed there waiting for bright Dawn.

"As soon as rose-fingered early Dawn appeared,   270
he lit a fire and milked his flock, one by one,

with a new-born placed beside each mother.
When this work was over, he once again   [310]
snatched two of my men and gorged himself.
After his meal, he easily rolled back
the huge rock door, drove his rich flock outside,
and set the stone in place, as one might put
a cap back on a quiver. Then Cyclops,
whistling loudly, drove his fat flocks away
towards the mountain. He left me there,   280
plotting a nasty scheme deep in my heart,
some way of gaining my revenge against him,
if Athena would grant me that glory.
My heart came up with what appeared to me
the best thing I could do. An enormous club
belonging to Cyclops was lying there
beside a stall, a section of green olive wood   [320]
he'd cut to carry with him once it dried.
To human eyes it seemed just like the mast
on a black merchant ship with twenty oars,   290
a broad-beamed vessel which can move across
the mighty ocean—that's how long and wide
that huge club looked. Moving over to it,
I chopped off a piece, six feet in length,
gave it to my companions, telling them
to smooth the wood. They straightened it, while I,
standing at one end, chipped and tapered it
to a sharp point. Then I picked up the stake
and set it in the blazing fire to harden.
That done, I placed it carefully to one side,   300
concealing it beneath some of the dung
which lay throughout the cave in massive piles.   [330]
Then I told my comrades to draw lots
to see which men would risk their lives with me—
when sweet sleep came upon the Cyclops,
we'd lift that stake and twist it in his eye.
The crew drew lots and picked the very men
I would have chosen for myself, four of them,
with me included as fifth man in the group.
In the evening he came back, leading on   310
his fine-skinned animals and bringing them
inside the spacious cave, every sheep and goat
in his rich flock—not leaving even one
out in the open courtyard. Perhaps he had

47

a sense of something wrong, or else a god
had given him an order. He picked up   [340]
and put his huge rock door in place, then sat
to milk each ewe and bleating goat,
one by one, setting beside each mother
one of her young. When this task was over,   320
he quickly seized two men and wolfed them down.
Then I moved up and stood at Cyclops' side,
holding in my hands a bowl of ivy wood
full of my dark wine. I said:

        'Cyclops,
 take this wine and drink it, now you've had
 your meal of human flesh, so you may know
 the kind of wine we had on board our ship,
 a gift of drink I was carrying for you,
 in hope you'd pity me and send me off
 on my journey home. But your savagery   330   [350]
 is something I can't bear. You cruel man,
 how will any of the countless other men
 ever visit you in future? How you act
 is so against all human law.'

         "I spoke.
He grabbed the cup and gulped down the sweet wine.
Once he'd swallowed, he felt such great delight,
he asked me for some more, a second taste.

 'Be kind and give me some of that again.
 And now, without delay tell me your name,
 so, as my guest, I can offer you a gift,   340
 something you'll like. Among the Cyclopes,
 grain-bearing earth grows clusters of rich grapes,
 which Zeus' rain increases, but this drink—
 it's a stream of nectar and ambrosia.'

"He spoke. So I handed him more fiery wine.   [360]
Three times I poured some out and gave it to him,
and, like a fool, he swilled it down. So then,
once the wine had addled Cyclops' wits,
I spoke these reassuring words to him:

 'Cyclops, you asked about my famous name.   350
 I'll tell you. Then you can offer me a gift,
 as your guest. My name is Nobody.

My father and mother, all my other friends—
they call me Nobody.'

   "That's what I said.
His pitiless heart replied:

     'Well, Nobody,
I'll eat all your companions before you
and have you at the end—my gift to you,   [370]
since you're my guest.'

     "As he said this,
he collapsed and toppled over on his back,
lying with his thick neck twisted to one side.   360
All-conquering sleep then overpowered him.
In his drunken state he kept on vomiting,
his gullet drooling wine and human flesh.
So then I pushed the stake deep in the ashes,
to make it hot, and spoke to all my men,
urging them on, so no one, in his fear,
would hesitate. When that stake of olive wood,
though green, was glowing hot, its sharp point
ready to catch fire, I walked across to it   [380]
and with my comrades standing round me   370
pulled it from the fire. And then some god
breathed powerful courage into all of us.
They lifted up that stake of olive wood
and jammed its sharpened end down in his eye,
while I, placing my weight at the upper end,
twisted it around—just as a shipwright
bores a timber with a drill, while those below
make it rotate by pulling on a strap
at either end, so the drill keeps moving—
that's how we held the red-hot pointed stake   380
and twisted it inside the socket of his eye.
Blood poured out through the heat—around his eye,
lids and brows were singed, as his eyeball burned—   [390]
its roots were crackling in fire. When a blacksmith
plunges a great axe or adze in frigid water
with a loud hissing sound, to temper it
and make the iron strong—that's how his eye
sizzled around the stake of olive wood.
His horrific screams echoed through the rock.
We drew back, terrified. He yanked the stake   390
out of his eye—it was all smeared with blood—

49

hurled it away from him, and waved his arms.
He started yelling out to near-by Cyclopes,
who lived in caves up on the windy heights,   [400]
his neighbours. They heard him shouting out
and came crowding round from all directions.
Standing at the cave mouth, they questioned him,
asking what was wrong:

                    'Polyphemus,
what's so bad with you that you keep shouting
through the immortal night and wake us up?   400
Is some mortal human driving off your flocks
or killing you by treachery or force?'

"From the cave mighty Polyphemus roared:

       'Nobody is killing me, my friends,
by treachery, not using any force.'

"They answered him—their words had wings:

                 'Well, then,
if nobody is hurting you and you're alone,   [410]
it must be sickness given by great Zeus,
one you can't escape. So say your prayers
to our father, lord Poseidon.'

             "With these words,   410
they went away, and my heart was laughing—
my cunning name had pulled off such a trick.
But Cyclops groaned, writhing in agony.
Groping with his hands he picked up the stone,
removed it from the door, and sat down there,
in the opening. He stretched out his arms,
attempting to catch anyone who tried
to get out with the sheep. In his heart,
he took me for a fool. But I was thinking
the best thing I could do would be to find   420
if somehow my crewmen and myself   [420]
could escape being killed. I wove many schemes,
all sorts of tricks, the way a man will do
when his own life's at stake—and we were faced
with a murderous peril right beside us.
To my heart the best plan was as follows:
in Cyclops' flocks the rams were really fat—
fine, large creatures, with thick fleecy coats

50

of deep black wool. I picked three at a time
and, keeping quiet, tied them up together,   430
with twisted willow shoots, part of the mat
on which the lawless monster Polyphemus
used to sleep. The middle ram carried a man.
The two on either side were for protection.   [430]
So for every man there were three sheep.
I, too, had my own ram, the finest one
in the whole flock by far. I grabbed its back
then swung myself under its fleecy gut,
and lay there, face upwards, with my fingers
clutching its amazing fleece. My heart was firm.   440
We waited there like that until bright Dawn.

"As soon as rose-fingered early Dawn appeared,
males in the flock trotted off to pasture,
while the females, who had not been milked
and thus whose udders were about to burst,
bleated in their pens. Their master, in great pain,   [440]
ran his hands across the backs of all his sheep
as they moved past him, but was such a fool,
he didn't notice how my men were tied
to their bellies underneath. Of that flock   450
my ram was the last to move out through the door,
weighed down by its thick fleece and my sly thoughts.
Mighty Polyphemus, as he stroked its back,
spoke to the animal:

                      'My lovely ram,
     why are you the last one in the flock
     to come out of the cave? Not once before
     have you ever lagged behind the sheep.
     No. You've always been well out in front,
     striding off to graze on tender shoots of grass
     and be the first to reach the river's stream.   460 [450]
     You're the one who longs to get back home,
     once evening comes, before the others.
     But now you're last of all. You must be sad,
     grieving for your master's eye, now blinded
     by that evil fellow with his hateful crew.
     That Nobody destroyed my wits with wine.
     But, I tell you, he's not yet escaped being killed.
     If only you could feel and speak like me—
     you'd tell me where he's hiding from my rage.

I'd smash his brains out on the ground in here,   470
sprinkle them in every corner of this cave,
and then my heart would ease the agonies
this worthless Nobody has brought on me.'   [460]

"With these words, he pushed the ram away from him,
out through the door. After the ram had moved
a short distance from the cave and courtyard,
first I got out from underneath its gut
and then untied my comrades. We rushed away,
driving off those rich, fat, long-legged sheep,
often turning round to look behind us,   480
until we reached our ship—a welcome sight
to fellow crewmen—we'd escaped being killed,
although they groaned and wept for those who'd died.
But I would not allow them to lament—
with a scowl I told everyone to stop.
I ordered them quickly to fling on board
the many fine-fleeced sheep and then set sail   [470]
across the salty sea. They climbed aboard
at once, took their places on the rowing bench,
and, sitting in good order in their rows,   490
struck the grey sea with their oars. But then,
when I was as far from land as a man's voice
can carry when he yells, I shouted out
and mocked the Cyclops:

                                        'Cyclops,
        it seems he was no weakling, after all,
        the man whose comrades you so wished to eat,
        using brute force in that hollow cave of yours.
        Your evil acts were bound to catch you out,
        you wretch—you didn't even hesitate
        to gorge yourself on guests in your own home.   500
        Now Zeus and other gods have paid you back.'

"That's what I said. It made his heart more angry.   [480]
He snapped off a huge chunk of mountain rock
and hurled it. The stone landed up ahead of us,
just by our ship's dark prow. As the stone sank,
the sea surged under it, waves pushed us back
towards the land, and, like a tidal flood,
drove us on shore. I grabbed a long boat hook
and pushed us off, encouraging the crew,
and, with a nod of my head, ordering them   510

to ply their oars and save us from disaster.
They put their backs into it then and rowed.   [490]
But when we'd got some distance out to sea,
about twice as far, I started shouting,
calling the Cyclops, although around me
my comrades cautioned me from every side,
trying to calm me down:

             'That's reckless.
Why are you trying to irritate that savage?
Just now he threw a boulder in the sea
and pushed us back on shore. We really thought   520
he'd destroyed us there. If he'd heard us speak
or uttering a sound, he'd have hurled down
another jagged rock and crushed our skulls,
the timbers on this ship, as well. He's strong,
powerful enough to throw this far.'

           "That's what they said.   [500]
But my warrior spirit didn't listen.
So, anger in my heart, I yelled again:

     'Cyclops, if any mortal human being
asks about the injury that blinded you,
tell them Odysseus destroyed your eye,   530
a sacker of cities, Laertes' son,
a man from Ithaca.'

           "After I'd said this,
he stretched out his hands to starry heaven
and offered this prayer to lord Poseidon:

     'Hear me, Poseidon, Enfolder of the Earth,
dark-haired god, if I truly am your son
and if you claim to be my father,
grant that Odysseus, sacker of cities,   [530]
a man from Ithaca, Laertes' son,
never gets back home. If it's his destiny   540
to see his friends and reach his native land
and well-built house, may he get back late
and in distress, after all his comrades
have been killed, and in someone else's ship.
May he find troubles in his house, as well.'

"That's what he prayed. The dark-haired god heard him.
Then Cyclops once again picked up a rock,

a much larger stone, swung it round, and threw it,
using all his unimaginable force.
It landed right behind the dark-prowed ship   550
and almost hit the steering oar. Its fall   [540]
convulsed the sea, and waves then pushed us on,
carrying our ship up to the further shore.

"We reached the island where our well-decked ships
were grouped together. Our comrades sat around them,
in great sorrow, always watching for us.
We rowed in, drove our ship up on the sand,
then climbed out through the surf. From the ship's hold
we unloaded Cyclops' flock and shared it out.
I took great care to see that all men there   560
received an equal part. But when the flock
was being divided up, my well-armed comrades   [550]
awarded me the ram, my special gift,
one just for me. I sacrificed that ram,
there on the shore, to Zeus, Cronos' son,
lord of the dark cloud, ruler of all,
offering him burnt pieces of the thigh.
But he did not care for my sacrifice.
Instead he started planning to destroy
all my well-decked ships and loyal comrades.   570

"As soon as rose-fingered early Dawn appeared,   [560]
I roused my shipmates, ordered them aboard.
They untied cables fastened to the sterns
and got in at once, moved to the rowing bench,
and sitting in good order in their rows,
they struck the grey sea with their oar blades.
So we sailed away from there, sad at heart,
happy to have avoided being destroyed,
although some dear companions had been killed."

BOOK TEN

X

AEOLUS, THE LAESTRYGONIANS, AND CIRCE

"Next we reached Aeolia, a floating island,
where Aeolus lived, son of Hippotas,
whom immortal gods hold dear.[1] Around it,
runs an impenetrable wall of bronze,
and cliffs rise up in a sheer face of rock.
His twelve children live there in the palace,
six daughters as well as six full-grown sons.
He gave the daughters to the sons in marriage,
and they are always at a banquet feasting,
beside their dear father and good mother,   10
with an infinite supply of tasty food.
We reached the splendid palace in the city,
and for one whole month he entertained me,
always asking questions about everything—
Troy, Argive ships, how Achaeans made it home—
and I told him all from start to finish.
When, for my part, I asked to take my leave
and told him he should send me on my way,
he denied me nothing and helped me go.
He gave me a bag made out of ox-hide,   20
flayed from an animal nine years of age,
and tied up in it all the winds that blow   [20]
from every quarter, for Cronos' son
has made Aeolus keeper of the winds,
and he could calm or rouse them, as he wished.
With a shining silver cord he lashed that bag
inside my hollow ship, so as to stop
even the smallest breath from getting out.
He also got a West Wind breeze to blow
to carry ships and men on their way home.   30

"For nine whole days and nights we held our course,
and on the tenth we glimpsed our native land.
We came in so close we could see the men   [30]
who tend the beacon fires. But then sweet Sleep
came over me—I was too exhausted.
All that time my hands had gripped the sail rope—

---

[1]This next stop on Odysseus' journey is apparently a small island to the north of Sicily.

I'd not let go of it or passed it on
to any shipmate, so that we'd get home
more quickly. But as I slept, my comrades
started talking to each other, claiming   40
I was taking gold and silver back with me,
gifts of Aeolus, brave son of Hippotas.
Glancing at the man who sat beside him,
one of them would say something like this:

    'It's not fair. Everyone adores this man
    and honours him, no matter where he goes,
    to any city, any land. From Troy
    he's taking a huge stash of glorious loot—   [40]
    but those of us who've been on the same trip
    are coming home with empty hands. And now,   50
    Aeolus, because he's a friend of his,
    has freely given him these presents.
    Come on, let's see how much gold and silver
    he has in his bag.'

                "As they talked like this,
my companions' greedy thoughts prevailed.
They untied the bag. All the winds rushed out—
storm winds seized them, swept them out to sea,
in tears, away from their own native land.
At that point I woke up. Deep in my heart   [50]
I was of two minds—I could jump overboard   60
and drown at sea or just keep going in silence,
remain among the living. I stayed there
and suffered on. Covering up my head,
I lay down on the deck, while our ships,
loaded with my whimpering companions,
were driven by those vicious blasts of wind
all the way back to Aeolus' island.

"I set off for Aeolus' splendid palace.
I found him feasting with his wife and children.   [60]
So we went into the house and sat down   70
on the threshold, right beside the door posts.
In their hearts they were amazed. They asked me:

    'Odysseus, how is it you've come back here?
    We took great care to send you on your way
    so you'd get home, back to your native land."

"That's what they asked. With a heavy heart,
I answered them:

               'My foolish comrades,
aided by malicious Sleep, have injured me.
But, my friends, you can repair all this—
that's in your power.'

                   "I said these words   80   [70]
to reassure them. But they stayed silent.
Then their father gave me this reply:

     'Of all living men, you are the worst—
so you must leave this island with all speed.
It would violate all sense of what is right
if I assisted or escorted on his way
a man the blessed gods must hate. So leave.
You're here because deathless gods despise you.'

"Once he'd said this, he sent me from his house,
for all my heavy groans. Then, sick at heart,   90
we sailed on further, my crewmen's spirits
worn down by the weary work of rowing.
Because we'd been such fools, there was no breeze
to help us on our way. We went on like this
for six whole days and nights. On the seventh   [80]
we came to Telepylus, great citadel
of Lamus, king of Laestrygonians,
into a lovely harbour, with a sheer cliff
around it on both sides. Jutting headlands
facing one another extended out   100
beyond the harbour mouth, a narrow entrance.   [90]
All my shipmates brought their curved ships up
and moored them inside the hollow harbour
in a tightly clustered group—in that spot
there were never any waves, large or small.
Everything was calm and bright around them.
But I moored my black ship all by itself
outside the harbour, right against the land,
tying it to the rock. I clambered up the cliff
and stood there, on a rugged outcrop,   110
looking round. I could see no evidence
of human work or ploughing, only smoke
rising from the land. I sent some comrades out   [100]
to learn what the inhabitants were like.

They left the ships and came to a smooth road,
which wagons used to haul wood to the town
from high mountain slopes. Outside the city
they met a young girl collecting water,
the noble daughter of Antiphates,
a Laestrygonian. They asked the girl   120
who ruled the people here and who they were.   [110]
She quickly pointed out her father's lofty home.
They reached the splendid house and found his wife,
a gigantic woman, like a mountain peak.
They were appalled. She summoned her husband,
strong Antiphates, out of a meeting,
and he arranged a dreadful death for them—
he seized one of my shipmates and prepared
to make a meal of him. The other two
jumped up, ran off, and rushed back to the ships.   130
Antiphates then raised a hue and cry
throughout the city. Once they heard his call,
the powerful Laestrygonians poured out,
thronging in countless numbers from all sides—
not like men at all, but Giants. From cliffs   [120]
they hurled rocks down on us, the largest stones
a man can lift. The clamour rising from the ships
was dreadful—men were being destroyed,
ships were smashing into one another,
with those monsters spearing men like fish,   140
and taking them to eat a gruesome meal.
While they were slaughtering the sailors there,
trapped in the deep harbour, I grabbed my sword,
pulled it from my thigh, and cut the cables
on my dark-prowed ship, shouting at my crew,
ordering them to put their oars to work,
so we could get away from this disaster.
They all churned the water with their oar-blades,   [130]
terrified of being killed. We were relieved,
as my ship left the beetling cliffs behind,   150
moving out to sea. But all the other ships,
moored together in the harbour, were destroyed.

"We sailed on from there with heavy hearts,
until we reached the island of Aeaea,
where fair-haired Circe lived, fearful goddess.
Here, in silence, we brought our ship to land   [140]

inside a harbour with fine anchorage.
Some god was guiding us. Then we disembarked
and laid up in that spot two days and nights,
our hearts consumed with weariness and pain.   160

"As soon as rose-fingered early Dawn appeared,
I called a meeting and addressed them all:

    'Shipmates, let's quickly put our heads together
    to see if we have any options left.
    I don't think we do. I climbed a rocky crag,
    and from that vantage point spied out the land.
    It's an island with deep water round it,
    low-lying and flat. I saw with my own eyes
    smoke rising in the middle of the island,
    through dense brush and trees.'

                              "That's what I said.   170
But their spirits fell, as they remembered
what Laestrygonian Antiphates had done
and the violence of great Polyphemus,   [200]
that man-eating cyclops. They wept aloud,
shedding frequent tears. But their laments
were not much help to us. So I split up
my well-armed comrades in two separate groups,
each with its own leader. I commanded one,
and godlike Eurylochus led the other.
We shook our tokens in a bronze helmet.   180
When brave Eurylochus' lot fell out,
he set off with twenty-two companions,
all in tears, leaving us behind to grieve.
In a forest clearing they found Circe's house—   [210]
built of polished stone, with views in all directions.
There were mountain wolves and lions round it,
all bewitched by Circe's wicked potions.
But these beasts made no attack against my men.
Instead they stood on their hind legs and fawned,
wagging their long tails. Just as dogs will beg   190
around their master when he comes from dinner—
since he keeps bringing scraps to please their hearts—
that's how the wolves and sharp-clawed lions there
kept fawning round those men, who were afraid
just looking at those fearful animals.
They stood in fair-haired Circe's gateway   [220]

and heard her sweet voice singing in the house,
as she went back and forth before her loom,
weaving a huge, immortal tapestry,
the sort of work which goddesses create,   200
finely woven, luminous, and beautiful.
They all started shouting, calling her.
She came out at once, opened the bright doors,
and asked them in. In their foolishness,
they all accompanied her. Eurylochus   [230]
was the only one who stayed outside—
he thought it could be something of a trick.
She led the others in and sat them down
on stools and chairs, then made them a drink
of cheese and barley meal and yellow honey   210
stirred into Pramnian wine. But with the food
she mixed a vicious drug, so they would lose
all memories of home. Once they drank down
the drink she gave them, she took her wand,
struck each man, then penned them in her pigsties.
They had bristles, heads, and voices just like pigs—
their bodies looked like swine—but their minds   [240]
were as before, unchanged. In their pens they wept.
In front of them Circe threw down feed,
acorns, beech nuts, cornel fruit, the stuff   220
pigs eat when they are wallowing in mud.
Eurylochus came back immediately
to our swift black ship, bringing a report
of his comrades' bitter fate, eyes full of tears.
I slung my large bronze silver-studded sword
across my shoulder, grabbed my bow, and left.
But while I was moving through the sacred groves
on my way to Circe's home, a goddess
skilled in many magic potions, I met
Hermes of the Golden Wand. I was going   230
toward the house. He looked like a young man
when the first growth of hair is on his lip,
the age when youthful charm is at its height.
He gripped my hand, spoke to me, and said: [280]

'Your comrades, over there in Circe's house,
are penned up like swine in narrow stalls.
Are you intending now to set them free?
I don't think you'll make it back yourself—

you'll stay there with the rest of them. But come,
I'll keep you free from harm and save you.   240
Here, take a remedial potion with you.
Go in Circe's house. It's a protection
and will clear your head of any dangers
this day brings. She won't have power
to cast a spell on you. This fine potion,
which I'll provide you, will not allow it.

"After saying this, the Killer of Argus
pulled a herb out of the ground, gave it to me,
and explained its features. Its roots were black,
the flower milk-white. Moly the gods call it.   250
Then Hermes left, through the wooded island,
bound for high Olympus. I continued on
to Circe's home. As I kept going, my heart
was turning over many gloomy thoughts.
Once I'd made it over to the gateway   [310]
of fair-haired Circe's house, I just stood there
and called out. The goddess heard my voice.
She came out at once, opened her bright doors,
and asked me in. So I went in with her,
heart full of misgivings. She led me in   260
and sat me on a silver-studded chair,
a lovely object, beautifully made,
with a stool underneath to rest my feet.
She mixed her potion in a golden cup
for me to drink. In it she placed the drug,
her heart still bent on mischief. She offered it,
and, when I'd drunk it, without being bewitched,
she struck me with her wand and said these words:

'Off now to your sty, and lie down in there   [320]
with the rest of your companions.'   270

                              "She spoke.
But I pulled out the sharp sword on my thigh
and charged at Circe, as if I meant to kill her.
She gave a piercing scream, ducked, then ran up
and clasped my knees. Through her tears she spoke—
her words had wings:

                              'What sort of man are you?
Where are you from? Where is your city?
Your parents? I'm amazed you drank this drug

and were not bewitched. No other man
who's swallowed it has been able to resist,
once it's passed the barrier of his teeth.   280
In that chest of yours your mind holds out
against my spell. You must be Odysseus,   [330]
that resourceful man. The Killer of Argus,
Hermes of the Golden Wand, always told me
Odysseus in his swift black ship would come
on his way back from Troy. Come, put that sword
back in its sheath, and let the two of us
go up into my bed. When we've made love,
then we can trust each other.'

              "Once she said this,
I answered her and said:

                      'O Circe,   290
how can you ask me to be kind to you?
In your own home you've changed my crew to pigs
and keep me here. You're plotting mischief now,
inviting me to go up to your room,   [340]
into your bed, so when I have no clothes,
you can do me harm, destroy my manhood.
But I won't agree to climb into your bed,
unless, goddess, you'll agree to swear
a solemn oath that you'll make no more plans
to injure me with some new mischief.'   300

"When I'd said this, she made the oath at once,
as I had asked, that she'd not harm me.
Once she had sworn and finished with the oath,
I went up with Circe to her splendid bed.

"Meanwhile four women serving in her home
were busy in the hall, children of springs,   [350]
groves, and sacred rivers flowing to the sea.
One of them threw lovely purple coverlets
across the chairs and spread linen underneath.
Another pulled silver tables over to each chair   310
and then placed silver baskets on them.
The third one mixed deliciously sweet wine
inside a silver bowl, then served it out
in cups of gold. The fourth brought water in,
lit a large fire under a huge cauldron,
and warmed the water up until it boiled

inside the shining bronze. She sat me in a tub,   [360]
then, diluting water from that cauldron
so it was right for me, gave me a bath,
pouring water on my head and shoulders,   320
until the weariness that sapped my spirit
had left my limbs. After bathing me,
she rubbed me with rich oil, then dressed me
in a fine cloak and tunic and led me
to a handsome chair embossed with silver,
finely crafted, with a footstool underneath.
A servant brought a lovely golden jug,
poured water out into a silver basin,
so I could wash, and set a polished table   [370]
at my side. Then the worthy steward   330
brought in bread and set it there before me,
placing with it large quantities of food,
given freely from her stores. She bid me eat.
But in my heart I had no appetite.
So I sat there, thinking of other things,
my spirit sensing something ominous.
When Circe noticed me just sitting there,
not reaching for the food, weighed down with grief,
she came up close and spoke winged words to me:

     'Odysseus, why are you sitting here like this,   340
     like someone who can't speak, eating out your heart,
     never touching food or drink? Do you think
     this is another trick? You don't need to fear—   [380]
     I've already made a solemn promise
     I won't injure you.'

               "When she said this,
I answered her and said:

                  'O Circe,
     What man with any self-respect would start
     to eat and drink before he had released
     his shipmates and could see them face to face?
     If you are being sincere in asking me   350
     to eat and drink, then set my comrades free,
     so my own eyes can see my trusty crew.'

"When I'd said this, Circe went through the hall,
her wand clutched in her hand, and opened up
the pig-sty doors. She drove the herd out.

They looked like full-grown pigs, nine years old,   [390]
standing in front of her. She went through them,
smearing on each one another potion.
Those bristles brought on by that nasty drug
which they'd received from Circe earlier   360
fell from their limbs, and they were men again,
more youthful and much taller than before,
more handsome to the eye. Now they knew me.
Each man grabbed my hand, and all of them
were overcome with passionate weeping,
so the house around them echoed strangely.
Circe herself was moved to pity then—
standing close to me, the lovely goddess said: [400]

     'Son of Laertes, resourceful Odysseus,
     born from Zeus, go now to the sea shore,   370
     back to your swift ship, drag it up on land,
     and stash your goods and all equipment
     in the caves. Then come back here in person,
     and bring your loyal companions with you.'

"Her words persuaded my proud heart. I left,
going back to our swift ship beside the sea.
I found my trusty comrades at the ship
lamenting miserably, shedding many tears.
Just as on a farm calves frisk around the herd   [410]
when cows, having had their fill of grazing,   380
return back to the yard—they skip ahead,
and pens no longer hold them, as they run,
mooing in a crowd around their mothers,
that's how my shipmates, once they saw me,
thronged around, weeping—in their hearts it felt
as if they they'd got back to their native land,
the rugged town of Ithaca itself."

"Meanwhile, Circe had been acting kindly
to the rest of my companions in her home.
She'd given them baths, rubbed them with rich oil,   390 [450]
and dressed them in warm cloaks and tunics.
We found them all quite cheerful, eating
in the hall. When my men saw each other
and recognized their shipmates face to face,
their crying and moaning echoed through the house.
The lovely goddess came to me and said:

'Resourceful Odysseus, Laertes' son,
come now, eat my food, and drink my wine,   [460]
until you've got back that spirit in your chest
you had when you first left your native land   400
of rugged Ithaca. You're exhausted now—
you have no spirit when you're always brooding
on your painful wanderings. There's no joy
inside your heart—you've been through so much.'

"Our proud hearts were persuaded by her words.
We stayed there, day by day, for one whole year,
feasting on sweet wine and large supplies of meat.
But as the months and seasons came and went,
long spring days returned. A year had passed.   [470]
My trusty comrades summoned me and said: 410

'You god-driven man, now the time has come
to think about your native land once more,
if you are fated to be saved and reach
your high-roofed home and your own country.'

"My proud heart was persuaded by their words.
So all day long until the sun went down,
we sat there, feasting on huge amounts of meat
and on sweet wine. Once the sun had set
and darkness came, they lay down to sleep
in the shadowy hall. I went to Circe,   420 [480]
in her splendid bed, and clasped her knees.
The goddess listened to me as I begged,
speaking these winged words to her:

'Circe, grant me the promise which you made
to send me home. My spirit's keen to leave,
as are the hearts in my companions, too,
who, as they grieve around me, drain my heart,
whenever you are not there among us.'

"I spoke. The lovely goddess answered me at once.

'Resourceful Odysseus, Laertes' son   430
and Zeus' child, if it's against your will,
you should not now remain here in my house.
But first you must complete another journey—   [490]
to the home of Hades and dread Persephone.
Consult the shade of that Theban prophet,
blind Teiresias. His mind is unimpaired.

65

Even though he's dead, Persephone
has granted him the power to understand—
the others flit about, mere shadows.'

"As Circe finished, my spirit was breaking.   440
I sat weeping on her bed, for my heart
no longer wished to live or glimpse the daylight.
But when I'd had enough of shedding tears
and rolling in distress, I answered her: [500]

'Circe, who'll be the guide on such a journey?
No one ever sailed a black ship down to Hades.'

"The lovely goddess gave me a quick answer:

'Resourceful Odysseus, Laertes' son
and Zeus' child, don't concern yourself
about a pilot for your ship. Raise the mast,   450
spread your white sail, and just take your seat.
Then the breath of North Wind Boreas
will take you on your way. But once your ship
crosses flowing Oceanus, drag it ashore
at Persephone's groves, on the level beach
where tall poplars grow, willows shed their fruit,   [510]
right beside deep swirling Oceanus.[1]
Then you must go to Hades' murky home.
There Periphlegethon and Cocytus,
a stream which branches off the river Styx,   460
flow into Acheron. There's a boulder
where these two foaming rivers meet. Go there,
heroic man, and follow my instructions—
move close and dig a hole there two feet square.[2]
Pour libations to the dead around it,
first with milk and honey, next sweet wine,
and then a third with water. And shake out   [520]
white barley meal. Then pray there in earnest
to many powerless heads of those who've died,
with a vow that, when you reach Ithaca,   470
at home, you'll sacrifice a barren heifer,
the best you have, and will cram the altar

---

[1]Oceanus or Ocean is a river which in Homeric geography surrounds the lands and
the sea—it is, as it were, the outer rim of the world (which is flat).

[2]The Greek reads "as great as the length of a pugon [the distance from the elbow to
the first finger joints] here and there," about two feet.

with fine gifts, and that you'll make an offering
to Teiresias, a black ram just for him,
the finest creature in your flocks. And then,
when you've offered prayers of supplication
to celebrated nations of the dead,
you must sacrifice a ram and a black ewe,
twisting their heads down towards Erebus,
while you turn to face the flowing rivers,   480
looking backwards.[1] At that point many spirits
will emerge—they're the shadows of the dead.   [530]
Then call your crew. Tell them to flay and burn
the sheep lying there, killed by pitiless bronze.
Pray to the gods, to powerful Hades
and dread Persephone. Then from your thigh,
you must yourself draw out that sharp sword,
and, sitting there, prevent the powerless heads
of those who've died from coming near the blood,
until you have listened to Teiresias.'   490 [540]

"Circe finished. Dawn soon came on her golden throne.
The nymph then dressed me in a cloak and tunic
and clothed her body in a long white robe,
a lovely, finely woven garment, and tied
a splendid golden belt around her waist.
On her head she placed a veil. Then I went
through her house, rousing my companions,
going up to each man and reassuring him:

'No more sleeping now, no sweet slumbering.
Let's go. Queen Circe's told me what to do.'   500

"That's what I said. And their proud hearts agreed."   [550]

---

[1]Erebus is the deepest pit of Hades.

BOOK ELEVEN

XI
ODYSSEUS MEETS THE SHADES OF THE DEAD

"When we reached our boat down on the beach,
we dragged it out into the glittering sea,
set up the mast and sail in our black ship,
led on the sheep, and then embarked ourselves.
All day long, the sail stayed full, and we sped on
across the sea, until the sun went down
and all sea routes grew dark. Our ship then reached
the boundaries of deep-flowing Oceanus,
a region always wrapped in mist and cloud.
We sailed in there, dragged our ship on land,   10   [20]
and walked along the stream of Oceanus,
until we reached the place Circe described.

"Perimedes and Eurylochus held the sheep,
our sacrificial victims, while I unsheathed
the sharp sword on my thigh and dug a hole,
two feet each way. I poured out libations
to all the dead—first with milk and honey,
then sweet wine, and then a third with water.
Around the pit I sprinkled barley meal.
Then to the powerless heads of the departed   20
I offered many prayers, with promises
I'd sacrifice, once I returned to Ithaca,
a barren heifer in my home. With prayers and vows
I called upon the families of the dead.
Next I held the sheep above the hole
and slit their throats. Dark blood flowed down.

"Then out of Erebus came swarming up
shades of the dead—brides, young unmarried men,
old ones worn out with toil, young tender girls,
with hearts still new to sorrow, and many men   30
wounded by bronze spears, who'd died in war,   [40]
still in their blood-stained armour. Crowds of them
came thronging in from all sides of the pit,
with amazing cries. Pale fear took hold of me.
Then I called my comrades, ordering them
to flay and burn the sheep still lying there,
slain by cruel bronze, and pray to the gods,
to mighty Hades and dread Persephone.
And then I drew the sharp sword on my thigh

68

and sat there, stopping the powerless heads   40
of all the dead from getting near the blood,
until I'd asked Teiresias my questions.   [50]

"Then appeared the ghost of my dead mother,
Anticleia, brave Autolycus' daughter.
I'd left her still alive when I set off
for sacred Troy. Once I caught sight of her,
I wept, and I felt pity in my heart.
But still, in spite of all my sorrow,
I could not let her get too near the blood,
until I'd asked Teiresias my questions.   50

"Then came the shade of Teiresias from Thebes,   [90]
holding a golden staff. He knew who I was
and started speaking:

        'Resourceful Odysseus,
Laertes' son and Zeus' child, what now,
you unlucky man? Why leave the sunlight,
come to this joyless place, and see the dead?
Move from the pit and pull away your sword,
so I may drink the blood and speak the truth.'

"Teiresias finished talking. I drew back
and thrust my silver-studded sword inside its sheath.   60
When the blameless prophet had drunk dark blood,
he said these words to me:

        'Glorious Odysseus,   [100]
you ask about your honey-sweet return.
But a god will make your journey bitter.
As soon as you've escaped the dark blue sea
and reached the island of Thrinacia
in your sturdy ship, you'll find grazing there
the cattle and rich flocks of Helios,
who hears and watches over everything.
If you leave them unharmed and keep your mind   70   [110]
on your return, you may reach Ithaca,
though you'll have trouble. But if you touch them,
then I foresee destruction for your crew,
for you, and for your ship. And even if
you yourself escape, you'll get home again
in distress and late, in someone else's ship,
after losing every one of your companions.

There'll be trouble in your home—arrogant men
eating up your livelihood and wooing
your godlike wife by giving courtship gifts.   80
But when you come, you'll surely take revenge
for all their violence. Once you have killed
the suitors in your house with your sharp sword,   [120]
by cunning or in public, then take up
a well-made oar and go, until you reach
a people who know nothing of the sea,
who don't put salt on any food they eat,
and have no knowledge of ships painted red
or well-made oars that serve those ships as wings.
I'll tell you a sure sign you won't forget—   90
when someone else runs into you and says
you've got a shovel used for winnowing
on your broad shoulders. Then fix that fine oar
in the ground there, and make rich sacrifice   [130]
to lord Poseidon with a ram, a bull,
and a boar that breeds with sows. Then leave.¹
Go home, and there make sacred offerings
to the immortal gods, who hold wide heaven,
to all of them in order. Your death will come
far from the sea, such a gentle passing,   100
when you are bowed down with a ripe old age,
and your people prospering around you.
In all these things I'm telling you the truth.'²

"He finished speaking. Then I replied and said:

'Teiresias, no doubt the gods themselves
have spun the threads of this. But come, tell me—   [140]
and speak the truth—I can see there the shade
of my dead mother, sitting near the blood,
in silence. She does not dare confront

¹These remarks seem to suggest that Odysseus must finally propitiate Poseidon by
going somewhere far inland, where people have never heard of that god and, in
effect, make him known with the oar planted in the ground and a sacrifice. The
winnowing shovel is a device for separating grain from chaff.

²This prophecy of the death of Odysseus has prompted much comment, especially
the phrase "far from the sea," which some interpreters wish to emend to "from the
sea" (i.e., someone will arrive by boat and bring about Odysseus' death). It is
difficult to reconcile the idea of Odysseus being far from the sea with the mention
of his people (i.e., those in Ithaca) living well all around him, unless, as some
legends have it, he leaves Ithaca and becomes a ruler somewhere else.

the face of her own son or speak to him.   110
Tell me, my lord, how she may understand
just who I am.'

                    "When I'd finished speaking,
Teiresias quickly gave me his reply:

'I'll tell you so your mind will comprehend.
It's easy. Whichever shadow of the dead
you let approach the blood will speak to you
and tell the truth, but those you keep away
will once again withdraw.'

                    "After saying this,   [150]
the shade of lord Teiresias returned
to Hades' home, having made his prophecy.   120
But I stayed there undaunted, till my mother
came and drank dark blood. Then she knew me.
Full of sorrow, she spoke out—her words had wings:

'My son, how have you come while still alive
down to this sad darkness? For living men
it's difficult to come and see these things—
huge rivers, fearful waters, stand between us,
first and foremost Oceanus, which no man
can cross on foot. He needs a sturdy ship.
Have you only now come here from Troy,   130 [160]
after a long time wandering with your ship
and your companions? Have you not reached
Ithaca, nor seen your wife in your own home?'

"Once she'd finished, I answered her:

                    'Mother,
I had to come down here to Hades' home,
meet the shade of Teiresias of Thebes,
and hear his prophecy. I have not yet
come near Achaea's shores or disembarked
in our own land. I've been wandering round
in constant misery, ever since I left   140
with noble Agamemnon, bound for Troy,
to fight against the Trojans. But come now,
tell me—and make sure you speak the truth—   [170]
what grievous form of death destroyed you?
A lingering disease, or did archer Artemis
attack and kill you with her gentle arrows?

71

And tell me of my father and my son,
whom I left behind. Tell me of the wife
I married. What are her thoughts and plans?
Is she still there with her son, keeping watch   150
on everything? Or has she been married
to the finest of Achaeans?'

           "When I'd said this,   [180]
my honoured mother answered me at once:

'You can be sure she's waiting in your home,
her heart still faithful. But her nights and days
all end in sorrow, with her shedding tears.
As for your father, he stays on his farm
and never travels down into the town.
There he lies in sorrow, nursing in his heart
enormous grief, longing for your return.   160
A harsh old age has overtaken him.
That's how I met my fate and died, as well.
I was not attacked and killed in my own home
by gentle arrows of the keen-eyed archer,
nor did I die of some disease which takes   [200]
the spirit from our limbs, as we waste away
in pain. No. It was my longing for you,
glorious Odysseus, for your loving care,
that robbed me of my life, so honey sweet.'

"She finished. I considered how in my heart   170
I wished to hold the shade of my dead mother.
Three times my spirit prompted me to grasp her,
and I jumped ahead. But each time she slipped
out of my arms, like a shadow or a dream.
The pain inside my heart grew even sharper.
Then I spoke to her—my words had wings:

'Mother, why do you not wait for me?   [210]
I'd like to hold you, so that even here,
in Hades' home, we might throw loving arms
around each other and then have our fill   180
of icy lamentation. Or are you
just a phantom royal Persephone has sent
to make me groan and grieve still more?'

"I spoke. My honoured mother quickly said:

'My child, of all men most unfortunate,
no, Persephone, daughter of Zeus,
is not deceiving you. Once mortals die,
this is what's set for them. Their sinews
no longer hold the flesh and bone together.
The mighty power of blazing fire   190 [220]
destroys them, once our spirit flies from us,
from our white bones. And then it slips away,
and, like a dream, flutters to and fro.
But hurry to the light as quickly as you can.
Remember all these things, so later on
you can describe the details to your wife.'"

*[The shade of Odysseus' mother, Anticleia, leaves. Odysseus then
describes at length how he saw a large number of shades of famous
women from olden times.]*

Odysseus paused. All Phaeacians sat in silence,
saying not a word, spellbound in the shadowy hall.
The first to speak was white-armed Arete, who said:

"Phaeacians, how does this man seem to you   200
for beauty, stature, and within himself,
a fair, well-balanced mind? He is my guest,
though each of you shares in this honour, too.
So don't be quick to send him on his way,
and don't hold back your gifts to one in need."   [340]

Then old warrior Echeneus addressed them all—
one of the Phaeacian elders there among them:

"Friends, what our wise queen has just said to us,
as we'd expect, is not wide of the mark.
You must attend to her. But the last word   210
and the decision rest with Alcinous."

Once Echeneus finished, Alcinous spoke out:

"The queen indeed will have the final word,
as surely as I live and am the king
of the Phaeacians, men who love the oar.
But though our guest is longing to return,   [350]
let him try to stay until tomorrow.
By then I'll have completed all our gifts.
His leaving here is everyone's concern,
especially mine, since I control this land."   220

73

Resourceful Odysseus then replied to him and said:

"Lord Alcinous, of all men most renowned,
if you asked me to stay for one whole year,
to organize my escort and give splendid gifts,
then I would still agree. It's far better
to get back to one's own dear native land
with more wealth in hand. I'll win more respect,   [360]
more love from anyone who looks at me,
whenever I return to Ithaca."

Alcinous then answered him and said:

                   "Odysseus,   230
when we look at you, we do not perceive
that you're in any way a lying fraud,
like many men the black earth nourishes
and scatters everywhere, who make up lies
from things no man has seen. You speak so well,
and you have such a noble heart inside.
You've told your story with a minstrel's skill,   [370]
the painful agonies of all the Argives
and your own, as well. Come then, tell me this—
and speak the truth—did you see any comrades,   240
those godlike men who went with you to Troy
and met their fate there? This night before us
will be lengthy, astonishingly so.
It's not yet time to sleep here in the halls,
so tell me of these marvellous events."

Resourceful Odysseus then answered him
and said these words:

               "Lord Alcinous,
If you are eager to hear even more,   [380]
I will not hesitate to speak to you
of other things more pitiful than these.   250
I mean the troubles of those friends of mine
who perished later, who managed to escape
the Trojans frightening battle cries, but died
when they returned, thanks to the deviousness
of a malicious woman.

               "Once sacred Persephone
dispersed those female shadows here and there,
then the grieving shade of Agamemnon,

son of Atreus, appeared. Around him
other shades had gathered, all those who died
and met their fate alongside Agamemnon   260
in Aegisthus' house. He knew me at once.   [390]
When he'd drunk some blood, he wept aloud,
shedding many tears, stretching out his hands,
keen to reach me. But he no longer had
any inner power or strength, not like
the force his supple limbs possessed before.
I looked at him and wept. Pity filled my heart.
Then I spoke to him—my words had wings:

    'Lord Agamemnon, son of Atreus,
    king of men, what fatal net of grievous death   270
    destroyed you? Did Poseidon stir the winds   [400]
    into a furious storm and strike your ships?
    Or were you killed by enemies on land,
    while you were cutting out their cattle
    or rich flocks of sheep? Or were you fighting
    to seize their city and their women?'

"I paused, and he at once gave me his answer:

    'Resourceful Odysseus, Laertes' son,
    and Zeus' child, Poseidon didn't kill me
    in my ships by rousing savage winds   280
    into a vicious storm. Nor was I killed
    by enemies on land. No. Aegisthus
    brought on my fatal end. He murdered me,
    and he was helped by my accursed wife,   [410]
    after he'd invited me into his home
    and prepared a feast for me, like an ox
    one butchers in its stall. And so I died
    the most pitiful of deaths. Around me
    they kept killing the rest of my companions,
    like white-tusked pigs . The saddest thing I heard   290
    was Cassandra, Priam's daughter, screaming.
    That traitor Clytaemnestra slaughtered her
    right there beside me. Though I was dying,
    I raised my arms to strike her with my sword,
    but that dog-faced bitch turned her back on me.
    Even though I was on my way to Hades,

she made no attempt to use her fingers
to close my eyelids or to shut my mouth."[1]

"Agamemnon finished. I answered him at once:

'That's horrible. Surely wide-thundering Zeus   300
for many years has shown a dreadful hate
towards the family of Atreus,
thanks to the conniving of some woman.
Many died for Helen's sake, and then
Clytaemnestra organized a trap for you,
while you were somewhere far away.'[2]

"As we two stood there in sad conversation,
full of sorrow and shedding many tears,
Achilles' shade came up, son of Peleus,
with those of splendid Antilochus   310
and Patroclus, too, as well as Ajax,
who in his looks and body was the best
of all Danaans, after Achilles,   [470]
who had no equal. Then the shadow
of the swift-footed son of Aeacus
knew who I was, and with a cry of grief,
he spoke to me—his words had wings:[3]

'Resourceful Odysseus, Laertes' son
and Zeus' child, what a bold man you are!
What exploit will your heart ever dream up   320
to top this one? How can you dare to come
down into Hades' home, the dwelling place
for the mindless dead, shades of worn-out men?'

"Achilles spoke. I answered him at once:

'Achilles, son of Peleus, mightiest
by far of the Achaeans, I came here
because I had to see Teiresias.
He might tell me a plan for my return   [480]

---

[1]These actions were made out of respect for the dead on their way to the underworld. The refusal to carry them out shows the greatest disrespect. Cassandra, a princess of Troy, was a prize of war awarded by the army to Agamemnon.

[2]Helen was married to Menelaus, brother of Agamemnon. Hence, the war caused by her elopement with Paris brought trouble on the House of Atreus.

[3]This is a reference to Achilles. Aeacus was a son of Zeus and the father of Peleus, hence Achilles' grandfather.

to rugged Ithaca. I've not yet come near
Achaean land. I've still not disembarked   330
in my own country. I'm in constant trouble.
But as for you, Achilles, there's no man
in earlier days who was more blest than you,
and none will come in future. Before now,
while you were still alive, we Argives
honoured you as we did the gods. And now,
since you've come here, you rule with power
among those who have died. So Achilles,
you have no cause to grieve because you're dead.'

"I paused, and he immediately replied: 340

'Don't try to comfort me about my death,
glorious Odysseus. I'd rather live
working as a wage-labourer for hire
by some other man, one who had no land
and not much in the way of livelihood,   [490]
than lord it over all the wasted dead.'

*[Odysseus then gives Achilles news about the outstanding qualities
of Achilles' son, Neoptolemus.]*

"With these words the shade of swift Achilles
moved away with massive strides through meadows
filled with asphodel, rejoicing that I'd said
his son was such a celebrated man.   350   [540]

"The other shadows of the dead and gone
stood there in sorrow, all asking questions
about the ones they loved. The only one
who stood apart was the shade of Ajax,
son of Telamon, still full of anger
for my victory, when I'd bested him
beside our ships, in that competition
for Achilles' arms. His honoured mother
had offered them as prizes. The judges
were sons of Troy and Pallas Athena.[1]   360
How I wish I'd never won that contest!
Those weapons were the cause earth swallowed up

---

[1]When Achilles died there was a contest for his famous weapons. The two main
claimants were Odysseus and the Greater Ajax. When Odysseus was awarded the
weapons by the judges, Ajax went berserk and later killed himself.

the life of Ajax, such a splendid man,
who, in his looks and actions, was the best   [550]
of all Danaans after the noble son
of Peleus. I called to him—my words
were meant to reassure him:

                        'Ajax,
worthy son of Telamon, can't you forget,
even when you're dead, your anger at me
over those destructive weapons? The gods   370
made them a curse against the Argives,
when they lost you, such a tower of strength.
Now you've been killed, Achaeans mourn your death
unceasingly, just as they do Achilles,
son of Peleus. No one is to blame
but Zeus, who in his terrifying rage   [560]
against the army of Danaan spearmen
brought on your death. Come over here, my lord,
so you can hear me as I talk to you.
Let your proud heart and anger now relent.'   380

"I finished. He did not reply, but left,
moving off toward Erebus, to join
the other shadows of the dead and gone.
For all his anger, he would have talked to me,
or I to him, but in my chest and heart
I wished to see more shades of those who'd died.

"And I saw Tityus, son of glorious Earth,
lying on the ground. His body covered
nine acres and more. Two vultures sat there,
one on either side, ripping his liver,   390
their beaks jabbing deep inside his guts.[1]
His hands could not fend them off his body.
He'd assaulted Leto, Zeus' lovely wife   [580]
as she was passing through Panopeus,
with its fine dancing grounds, towards Pytho.

"Then I saw Tantalus in agony,
standing in a pool of water so deep
it almost reached his chin. He looked as if

---

[1]Tityus was a giant son of Zeus (or of Ouranos). Hera persuaded Tityus to attack
Leto, whose children, Apollo and Artemis, came to her help and killed him. The
measurement describing his size is unclear.

he had a thirst but couldn't take a drink.
Whenever that old man bent down, so keen   400
to drink, the water there was swallowed up
and vanished. You could see black earth appear
around his feet. A god dried up the place.
Some high and leafy trees above his head
were in full bloom—pears and pomegranates,
apple trees, all with gleaming fruit, sweet figs,   [590]
and luscious olives. Each time the old man
stretched out his arms to reach for them,
a wind would raise them to the shadowy clouds.[1]

"And then, in his painful torment, I saw   410
Sisyphus striving with both hands to raise
a massive rock.[2] He'd brace his arms and feet,
then strain to push it uphill to the top.
But just as he was going to get that stone
across the crest, its overpowering weight
would make it change direction. The cruel rock
would roll back down again onto the plain.
Then he'd strain once more to push it up the slope.
His limbs dripped sweat, and dust rose from his head.   [600]

"And then I noticed mighty Hercules,   420
or at least his image, for he himself
was with immortal gods, enjoying their feasts.[3]
Hebe with the lovely ankles is his wife,
daughter of great Zeus and Hera, goddess
of the golden sandals. Around him there
the dead were making noises, just like birds
fluttering to and fro quite terrified.
And like dark night, he was glaring round him,
his unsheathed bow in hand, with an arrow
on the string, as if prepared to shoot.   430

---

[1]Tantalus was a son of Zeus. His punishment is the result of some action he committed against the gods (stealing the gods' food or murdering his son Pelops and serving him to the gods for dinner).

[2]Sisyphus gave away the secrets of the gods and once tricked the god of death, so that the dead could not reach the underworld.

[3]Hercules, a mortal, had the rare distinction of being admitted to heaven after his death. Hence, Odysseus meets an "image" of Hercules. His later mention of serving an inferior man is a reference to the Labours of Hercules, work he had to carry out for king Eurystheus over a twelve-year period.

The strap across his chest was frightening,
a golden belt inlaid with images—   [610]
amazing things—bears, wild boars, and lions
with glittering eyes, battles, fights, and murders,
men being killed. I hope whoever made it,
the one whose skill conceived that belt's design,
never made or ever makes another.
His eyes saw me and knew just who I was.
With a mournful tone he spoke to me—
his words had wings:

                              'Resourceful Odysseus,   440
          son of Laertes and a child of Zeus,
          are you now bearing an unhappy fate
          below the sunlight, as I, too, did once?
          I was a son of Zeus, child of Cronos,
          and yet I had to bear countless troubles,   [620]
          forced to carry out labours for a man
          vastly inferior to me, someone
          who kept assigning me the harshest tasks.
          Once he sent me here to bring away
          Hades' hound. There was no other challenge   450
          he could dream up more difficult for me
          than that one. But I carried the dog off
          and brought him back from Hades with my guides,
          Hermes and gleaming-eyed Athena.'

"With these words he returned to Hades' home.
But I stayed at that place a while, in case
one of those heroic men who perished
in days gone by might come. I might have seen
still more men from former times, the ones   [630]
I wished to see—Theseus and Perithous,   460
great children of the gods. Before I could,
a thousand tribes of those who'd died appeared,
with an astounding noise. Pale fear gripped me—
holy Persephone might send at me
a horrific monster, the Gorgon's head.[1]
I quickly made my way back to the ship,
ordered my crew to get themselves on board,

---

[1]The Gorgons were three terrifying sisters (the most famous being Medusa, the only one who was not immortal, whose head, even when cut off, could turn men to stone).

and loosen off the cables at the stern.
They went aboard at once and took their seats
along each rowing bench. A rising swell   470
carried our ship down Oceanus' stream.
We rowed at first, but then a fair wind blew."   [640]

Book Twelve

XII

The Sirens, Scylla and Charybdis, the Cattle of the Sun

"Our ship sailed on, away from Ocean's stream,
across the great wide sea, and reached Aeaea,
the island home and dancing grounds of Dawn.[1]
We sailed in, hauled our ship up on the beach,
then walked along the shore beside the sea.
There, waiting for bright Dawn, we fell asleep.

"Circe was well aware of our return
from Hades' home. Dressed in her finery,
she quickly came to us. With her she brought
servants carrying bread, plenty of meat,   10
and bright red wine. Then the lovely goddess
stood in our midst and spoke to us: [20]

       'You reckless men,
 you've gone to Hades' home while still alive,
 to meet death twice, when other men die once.
 But come, eat this food and drink this wine.
 Take all day. As soon as Dawn arrives,
 you'll sail. I'll show you your course and tell you
 each sign to look for, so you'll not suffer,
 or, thanks to vicious plans of sea and land,
 endure great pain.'

      "Circe finished speaking.   20
And our proud hearts agreed with what she'd said.
So all that day until the sun went down
we sat there eating rich supplies of meat   [30]
and drinking down sweet wine. The sun then set,
and darkness came. So we lay down and slept
beside stern cables of our ship. But Circe
took me by the hand and led me off,
some distance from the crew. She made me sit,
while she lay there on the ground beside me.
I told her every detail of our trip,   30

---

[1]This return to Aeaea, Circe's island, is puzzling, because the description of it here seems to place in a very different location than earlier (in the east rather than in the west).

describing all of it from start to finish.
Then queen Circe spoke to me and said:

'All these things have thus come to an end.
But you must listen now to what I say—
a god himself will be reminding you.
First of all, you'll run into the Sirens.
They seduce all men who come across them   [40]
Whoever unwittingly goes past them
and hears the Sirens' call never gets back.
His wife and infant children in his home   40
will never stand beside him full of joy.
No. Instead, the Sirens' clear-toned song
will captivate his heart. They'll be sitting
in a meadow, surrounded by a pile,
a massive heap, of rotting human bones
encased in shrivelled skin. Row on past them.
Roll some sweet wax in your hand and stuff it
in your companions' ears, so none of them
can listen. But if you're keen to hear them,
make your crew tie you up to your swift ship.   50   [50]
When your crew has rowed on past the Sirens,
I cannot tell you which alternative
to follow on your route—for you yourself
will have to trust your heart. But I'll tell you
the options. One has overhanging rocks,
on which dark-eyed Amphitrite's great waves   [60]
smash with a roar. These cliffs the blessed gods
have called the Planctae. No birds pass through there.
No human ship has ever reached this place
and got away. Instead, waves from the sea   60
and destructive blasts of fire carry off
a whirling mass of timbers from the boat
and human bodies. Only one ocean ship,
most famous of them all, has made it through,
the Argo, sailing on her way from Aeetes,   [70]
and waves would soon have smashed that vessel, too,
against the massive rocks, had not Hera
sent her through. For Jason was her friend.[1]
On the other route there are two cliffs.

---

[1]The Argo is the ship which carried Jason and his companions to Colchis on their trip to capture the Golden Fleece and back again. Aeetes was king of Colchis.

One has a sharp peak jutting all the way   70
up to wide heaven. Around that mountain
a dark cloud sits, which never melts away.
No human being could climb up that rock
and stand on top. Half way up the rock face   [80]
there's a shadowy cave. It faces west,
towards Erebus. You'll steer your ship at it,
In there lives Scylla. She has a dreadful yelp.
It's true her voice sounds like a new-born pup,
but she's a vicious monster. Nobody
would feel good seeing her, nor would a god   80
who crossed her path. She has a dozen feet,
all deformed, six enormously long necks,   [90]
with a horrific head on each of them,
and three rows of teeth packed close together,
full of murky death. Her lower body
she keeps out of sight in her hollow cave,
but sticks her heads outside the fearful hole,
and fishes there, scouring around the rock
for dolphins, swordfish, or some bigger prey,
whatever she can seize of all those beasts   90
moaning Amphitrite keeps nourishing
in numbers past all counting. No sailors
can yet boast they and their ship sailed past her
without getting hurt. Each of Scylla's heads
carries off a man, snatching him away   [100]
right off the dark-prowed ship. Then, Odysseus,
you'll see the other cliff. It's not so high.
There's a huge fig tree there with leaves in bloom.
Just below that tree divine Charybdis
sucks black water down. She spews it out   100
three times a day, and then three times a day
she gulps it down—a terrifying sight.
May you never meet her when she swallows!
Nothing can save you from destruction then,
not even Poseidon, Shaker of the Earth.
Make sure your ship stays close to Scylla's rock.
Row past there quickly. It's much better
to mourn for six companions in your ship   [110]
than to have them all wiped out together.'

'Next you'll reach the island of Thrinacia,   110
where Helios' many cattle graze,

his rich flocks, too—seven herds of cattle
and just as many lovely flocks of sheep,
with fifty in each group. They bear no young   [130]
and never die. Their herders are divine.
Now, if you leave these animals unharmed
and focus on your journey home, I think
you may get back to Ithaca, although
you'll bear misfortunes. But if you harm them,
then I foresee destruction for your ship   120
and crew. Even if you yourself escape,   [140]
you'll get back home in great distress and late,
after all your comrades have been killed.'

"Circe finished speaking. When Dawn came up
on her golden throne, the lovely goddess
left to go up island. So I returned
back to the ship and urged my comrades
to get on board and loosen off the stern ropes.
They quickly climbed into the ship, sat down
in proper order at each rowing bench,   130
and struck the grey sea with their oars. Fair winds
began to blow behind our dark-prowed ship.
Then the wind died down. Everything was calm,
without a breeze. Some god had stilled the waves.
My comrades stood up, furled the sail, stowed it   [170]
in the hollow ship, and then sat at their oars,
churning the water white with polished blades
carved out of pine. With my sharp sword I cut
a large round chunk of wax into small bits,
then kneaded them in my strong fingers.   140
Once I'd plugged my comrades' ears with wax,
they tied me hand and foot onto the ship,
so I stood upright hard against the mast.
They lashed the rope ends to the mast as well,
then sat and struck the grey sea with their oars.   [180]
But when we were about as far away
as a man can shout, moving forward quickly,
our swift ship did not get past the Sirens,
once it came in close, without being noticed.
So they began their clear-toned cry:

                              'Odysseus,   150
you famous man, great glory of Achaeans,
come over here. Let your ship pause awhile,

85

so you can hear the songs we two will sing.
No man has ever rowed in his black ship
past this island and not listened to us,
sweet-voiced melodies sung from our lips.
That brings him joy, and he departs from here
a wiser man, for we two understand
all the things that went on there in Troy,
all Trojan and Achaean suffering, 160 [190]
thanks to what the gods then willed, for we know
all things that happen on this fertile earth.'

"They paused. The voice that reached me was so fine
my heart longed to listen. I told my crew
to set me free, sending them clear signals
with my eyebrows. But they fell to the oars
and rowed ahead. Then two of them got up,
Perimedes and Eurylochus, bound me
with more rope and lashed me even tighter.
Once they'd rowed on well beyond the Sirens, 170
my loyal crewmates quickly pulled out wax
I'd stuffed in each man's ears and loosed my ropes. [200]

"But once we'd left the island far behind,
I saw giant waves and smoke. Then I heard
a crashing roar. The men were terrified.
I went through the ship, cheering up the crew,
standing beside each man and speaking words
of reassurance:

   'Friends, up to this point,
we've not been strangers to misfortunes.
Surely the bad things now are nothing worse 180
than when the cyclops with his savage force [210]
kept us his prisoners in his hollow cave.
But even there, thanks to my excellence,
intelligence, and planning, we escaped.
I think someday we'll be remembering
these dangers, too. But come now, all of us
should follow what I say. Stay by your oars,
and keep striking them against the surging sea.
Zeus may somehow let us escape from here.'

"I spoke. They quickly followed what I'd said. 190
I didn't speak a word of Scylla—she was
a threat for which there was no remedy—

in case my comrades, overcome with fear,
might stop rowing and huddle together
inside the boat. We kept sailing on,
up the narrow strait, groaning as we moved.
On one side lay Scylla. On the other one
divine Charybdis terrified us all,
by swallowing salt water from the sea.
When she spewed it out, she seethed and bubbled   200
uncontrollably, just like a cauldron
on a massive fire, while high above our heads
spray was falling on top of both the cliffs.
When she sucked the salt sea water down,   [240]
everything in there looked totally confused,
a dreadful roar arose around the rocks,
and underneath the dark and sandy ground
was visible. Pale fear gripped my crewmen.
When we saw Charybdis, we were afraid
we'd be destroyed. Then Scylla snatched away   210
six of my companions, right from the ship,
the strongest and the bravest men I had.
When I turned to watch the swift ship and crew,
already I could see their hands and feet,
as Scylla carried them high overhead.
They cried out and screamed, calling me by name
one final time, their hearts in agony.   [250]
Then, in the entrance to her cave, Scylla
devoured the men, who still kept screaming,
stretching out their arms in my direction,   220
as they met their painful deaths. Of all things
my eyes have witnessed in my journeying
on pathways of the sea, the sight of them
was the most piteous I've ever seen.

"Once we'd made it past those rocks and fled,   [260]
escaping Scylla and dread Charybdis,
we reached the lovely island of the god,
home of those splendid broad-faced cattle
and numerous rich flocks belonging to
Helios Hyperion, god of the sun.   230
While I was still at sea in my black ship,
I heard the lowing cattle being penned
and bleating sheep. There fell into my heart
the speeches of Teiresias of Thebes,

the sightless prophet—Circe's words, as well,
on Aeaea. They had both strictly charged
that I should at all costs miss this island,
the property of Helios, who brings
such joy to men.

[Odysseus' men bitterly complain about avoiding the island, challenging his decision. Odysseus reluctantly decides to land there.]

        "So with a heavy heart   [270]
I spoke to my companions:

               'Comrades,   240
let all of you now swear this solemn oath—
if by chance we find a herd of cattle
or a large flock of sheep, not one of you   [300]
will be so overcome with foolishness
that you'll kill a cow or sheep. No. Instead,
you'll be content to eat the food supplies
which goddess Circe gave.'

           "Once I'd said this,
they swore, as I had asked, they'd never kill
those animals. When they had made the oath
and finished promising, we moved our ship   250
inside a hollow harbour, by a spring
whose water tasted sweet. Then my crewmen
disembarked and made a skillful dinner.
When everyone had eaten food and drunk
to his heart's ease, they wept as they recalled
those dear companions Scylla snatched away
out of the hollow ship and then devoured.   [310]
As they cried there, sweet sleep came over them.

"But when three-quarters of the night had passed
and the stars had shifted their positions,   260
cloud-gatherer Zeus stirred up a nasty wind
and an amazing storm, which hid in clouds
both land and sea alike. And from heaven
dark Night rushed down. Once rose-fingered Dawn arrived,
we dragged up our ship and made it secure
inside a hollow cave, a place nymphs used
as a fine dancing and assembly ground.
Then I called a meeting of the men and said:

'My friends, in our ship we have meat and drink,   [320]
so let's not touch those cattle, just in case   270
that causes trouble for us. For these cows
and lovely sheep belong to Helios,
a fearful god, who spies out all there is
and listens in on everything as well.'

"These words of mine won over their proud hearts.
But then South Wind kept blowing one whole month.
It never stopped. No other wind sprang up,
except those times when East or South Wind blew.
As long as the men had red wine and bread,
they didn't touch the cattle. They were keen   280
to stay alive. But once what we had stored
inside our ship was gone, they had to roam,
scouring around for game and fish and birds,   [330]
whatever came to hand. They used bent hooks
to fish, while hunger gnawed their stomachs.
At that point I went inland, up island,
to pray to the gods, hoping one of them
would show me a way home. Once I'd moved
across the island, far from my comrades,
I washed my hands in a protected spot,   290
a shelter from the wind, and said my prayers
to all the gods who hold Mount Olympus.
Then they poured sweet sleep across my eyelids.
Meanwhile Eurylochus began to give
disastrous advice to my companions:

'Shipmates, although you're suffering distress,   [340]
hear me out. For wretched human beings
all forms of death are hateful. But to die
from lack of food, to meet one's fate that way,
is worst of all. So come, let's drive away   300
the best of Helios' cattle, and then
we'll sacrifice to the immortal gods
who hold wide heaven. And if we get home,
make it to Ithaca, our native land,
for Helios Hyperion we'll build
a splendid temple, and inside we'll put
many wealthy offerings. If he's enraged
about his straight-horned cattle and desires
to wreck our ship and other gods agree,
I'd rather lose my life once and for all   310 [350]

89

choking on a wave than starving to death
on an abandoned island.'

               "Eurylochus spoke.
My other comrades agreed with what he'd said.
They quickly rounded up the finest beasts
from Helios' herd, which was close by,
sleek, broad-faced animals with curving horns
grazing near the dark-prowed ship. My comrades
stood around them, praying to the gods.
They broke off tender leaves from a high oak,
for there was no white barley on the ship.[1]   320
After their prayers, they cut the creatures' throats,
flayed them, and cut out portions of the thighs.
These they covered in a double layer of fat   [360]
and laid raw meat on top. They had no wine
to pour down on the flaming sacrifice,
so they used some water for libations
and roasted all the entrails in the fire.
Once the thigh parts were completely roasted
and they'd had a taste of inner organs,
they sliced up the rest and skewered it on spits.   330
That was the moment sweet sleep left my eyes.
I went down to our swift ship on the shore.
As I drew closer to our curving ship,
the sweet smell of hot fat floated round me.
I groaned and cried out to immortal gods: [370]

     'Father Zeus and you other sacred gods,
     who live forever, you forced it on me,
     that cruel sleep, to bring about my doom.
     For my companions who remained behind
     have planned something disastrous.'

              "A messenger   340
quickly came to Helios Hyperion,
long-robed Lampetie, bringing him the news—
we had killed his cattle. Without delay,
he spoke to the immortals, full of rage:

     'Father Zeus and you other blessed gods,
     who live forever, take your vengeance now

---

[1] The traditional sacrifice requires white barley. But since the sailors are out of food, they have to substitute the leaves for the barley.

on those companions of Odysseus,
Laertes' son, who, in their arrogance,
have killed my animals, the very ones
I always look upon with such delight   350 [380]
whenever I move up to starry heaven
and then turn back from there towards the earth.
If they don't pay me proper retribution
for those beasts, then I'll go down to Hades
and shine among the dead.'

          "Cloud-gatherer Zeus
answered him and said:

               'Helios, I think
you should keep on shining for immortals
and for human beings on fertile earth.
With a dazzling thunderbolt I myself
will quickly strike at that swift ship of theirs   360
and, in the middle of the wine-dark sea,
smash it to tiny pieces.'

          "I learned of this
from fair Calypso, who said she herself   [390]
had heard it from Hermes the Messenger.

"I came down to the sea and reached the ship.
Then I bitterly attacked my crewmen,
each of them in turn, standing by the boat.
But we couldn't find a single remedy—
the cattle were already dead. The gods
immediately sent my men bad omens—   370
hides crept along the ground, while on the spits
the meat began to bellow, and a sound
like cattle lowing filled the air.

          "For six days,
those comrades I had trusted feasted there,
eating the cattle they had rounded up,
the finest beasts in Helios' herd.
But when Zeus, son of Cronos, brought to us
the seventh day, the stormy winds died down.   [400]
We went aboard at once, put up the mast,
hoisted the white sail, and then set off,   380
out on the wide sea.

"Once we'd left that island,
no other land appeared, only sky and sea.
The son of Cronos sent us a black cloud,
above our hollow ship, while underneath
the sea grew dark. Our boat sailed on its course,
but not for long. All at once, West Wind whipped up
a frantic storm—the blasts of wind snapped off
both forestays on the mast, which then fell back,   [410]
and all our rigging crashed down in the hold.
In the stern part of the ship, the falling mast   390
struck the helmsman on his head, caving in
his skull, every bone at once. Then he fell,
like a diver, off the ship. His proud spirit
left his bones. Then Zeus roared out his thunder
and with a bolt of lightning struck our ship.
The blow from Zeus' lightning made our boat
shiver from stem to stern and filled it up
with sulphurous smoke. My crew fell overboard
and were carried in the waves, like cormorants,
around our blackened ship, because the god   400
had robbed them of their chance to get back home.
But I kept pacing up and down the ship,   [420]
until the breaking seas had loosened off
both sides of the keel. Waves were holding up
the shattered ship but then snapped off the mast
right at the keel. But the ox-hide backstay
had fallen over it, and so with that
I lashed them both together, mast and keel.
I sat on these and then was carried off
by those destructive winds. But when the storms   410
from West Wind ceased, South Wind began to blow,
and that distressed my spirit—I worried
about floating back to grim Charybdis.
All night I drifted. When the sun came up,
I reached Scylla's cliff and dread Charybdis   [430]
sucking down salt water from the sea.
But I jumped up into the high fig tree
and held on there, as if I were a bat.
But there was nowhere I could plant my feet,
nor could I climb the tree, so I hung there,   420
staunch in my hope that when she spewed again,
she'd throw up keel and mast. And to my joy
they finally appeared. My hands and feet let go

and from up high I fell into the sea
beyond those lengthy spars. I sat on them
and used my hands to paddle my way through.
As for Scylla, the father of gods and men
would not let her catch sight of me again,
or else I'd not have managed to escape
being utterly destroyed.

       "From that place   430
I drifted for nine days. On the tenth night,
the gods conducted me to Ogygia,
the island where fair-haired Calypso lives,
fearful goddess with the power of song.
She welcomed and took good care of me.   [450]
But why should I tell you that story now?
It was only yesterday, in your home,
I told it to you and your noble wife.
And it's an irritating thing, I think,
to re-tell a story once it's clearly told."   440

XIII
ODYSSEUS LEAVES PHAEACIA AND REACHES ITHACA

Odysseus paused. All Phaeacians sat in silence,
without saying a word, spellbound in the shadowy hall.
Then Alcinous again spoke up and said to him:

> "Odysseus, since you're visiting my home,
> with its brass floors and high-pitched roof, I think
> you won't leave here and go back disappointed,
> although you've truly suffered much bad luck.
> Clothing for our guest is packed already,   [10]
> stored in a polished chest inlaid with gold,
> as well as all the other gifts brought here   10
> by Phaeacia's counsellors."

                    Mighty Alcinous
dispatched a herald to conduct him to the sea
and his fast ship. Once they'd come down to the ship,   [70]
beside the sea, the noble youths accompanying him
immediately took all the food and drink on board
and stowed them in the hollow ship. They spread a rug
and linen sheet on the deck inside the hollow ship,
at the stern, so Odysseus could sleep in peace.
He went aboard, as well, and lay down in silence.
Each man sat in proper order at his oarlock.   20
They loosed the cable from the perforated stone.
Once they leaned back and stirred the water with their oars,
a calming sleep fell on his eyelids, undisturbed
and very sweet, something very similar to death.   [80]
Just as four stallions yoked together charge ahead
across the plain, all running underneath the lash,
and jump high as they gallop quickly on their way,
that's how the stern of that ship leapt up on high,
while in her wake the dark waves of the roaring sea
were churned to a great foam, as she sped on her path,   30
safe and secure. Not even a wheeling hawk,
the swiftest of all flying things, could match her speed,
as she raced ahead, slicing through the ocean waves,
carrying a man whose mind was like a god's.
His heart in earlier days had endured much pain,   [90]
when he moved through men's wars and suffered on the waves.
Now he slept in peace, forgetting all his troubles.

When the brightest of the stars rose up, the one
which always comes to herald light from early Dawn,
the sea-faring ship sailed in close to Ithaca.   40
Those rowers' arms had so much strength, half the boat,
which was moving fast, was driven up on shore.
Once they climbed out of that well-built rowing ship
onto dry land, first they took Odysseus out,
lifting him out of the hollow ship still wrapped up
in the linen sheet and splendid blanket, placed him,
fast asleep, down on the sand, then carried out
the gifts Phaeacia's noblemen had given him,   [120]
thanks to the goodwill of great-hearted Athena,
when he was setting out for home. They put these gifts   50
against the trunk of the olive tree, in a pile,
some distance from the path, in case someone came by,
before Odysseus could wake up, stumbled on them,
and robbed him. Then they set off, back to Phaeacia.

[Poseidon complains to Zeus about what the Phaeacians are doing
to help Odysseus, and Zeus tells him to punish them himself. So
Poseidon turns the Phaeacian ship and crew to stone, just as the
ship is about to reach home.]

Meanwhile, Odysseus, asleep in his own land,
woke up. He did not recognize just where he was.
And so all things seemed unfamiliar to their king,
the long straight paths, the harbour with safe anchorage,
the sheer-faced cliffs, the trees in rich full bloom.
So he jumped up and looked out at his native land.   60
He groaned aloud and struck his thighs with both his palms,
then expressed his grief, saying:

                              "Where am I now?   [200]
Whose country have I come to this time?
Are they violent, unjust, and cruel,
    or do they welcome strangers? Do their minds
respect the gods? And all this treasure here,
    where do I take that? Where do I go next?"

Then, overwhelmed with longing for his native land,
he wandered on the shore beside the crashing sea,   [220]
with many cries of sorrow. Then Athena came,   70
moving close to him in the form of a young man.
Odysseus, happy to catch sight of her, came up
and spoke to her—his words had wings:

"My friend,
since you're the first one I've encountered here,
tell me the truth, so I can understand—
What country is this? Who are these people?
Is it some sunny island or a headland
of the fertile mainland reaching out to sea?"

Athena, goddess with the gleaming eyes, replied:

"Stranger, you're a fool, or else you've come   80
from somewhere far away, if you must ask
about this land. Its name is not unknown—
not at all—many men have heard of it.
The name of Ithaca is known even in Troy,
a long way from Achaean land, they say."

Athena spoke, and much-enduring lord Odysseus   [250]
felt great joy, happy to learn of his ancestral lands.
Bright-eyed Athena smiled and stroked him with her hand.
Then she changed herself into a lovely woman,
tall and very skilled in making splendid things.   90
She spoke to him—her words had wings: [290]

"Odysseus,
of all men you're the best at making plans
and giving speeches, and among all gods
I'm well known for subtlety and wisdom.
Still, you failed to recognize Pallas Athena,   [300]
daughter of Zeus, who's always at your side,
looking out for you in every crisis.
Yes, I made all those Phaeacians love you.
Now I've come to weave a scheme with you
and hide these goods Phaeacian noblemen   100
gave you as you were setting out for home,
thanks to my plans and what I had in mind.
I'll tell you what Fate has in store for you.
You'll find harsh troubles in your well-built home.
Be patient, for you must endure them all.
Don't tell anyone, no man or woman,
you've returned from wandering around.
Instead, keep silent. Bear the many pains,
and, when men act savagely, do nothing.   [310]
Now, let's not delay, but put away these goods   110
in some hidden corner of this sacred cave,
where they'll stay safely stored inside for you.

And then let's think about how all these things
may turn out for the best."

After saying this,
the goddess went into the shadowy cave
and looked around for hiding places. Odysseus
brought in all the treasures—enduring bronze and gold
and finely woven clothes, gifts from the Phaeacians.
He stored these carefully, and Pallas Athena,   [370]
daughter of aegis-bearing Zeus, set a rock in place   120
to block the entranceway.

Then the two of them
sat down by the trunk of the sacred olive tree
to think of ways to kill those arrogant suitors.
Bright-eyed goddess Athena was the first to speak:

"Resourceful Odysseus, Laertes' son
and child of Zeus, think how your hands may catch
these shameless suitors, who for three years now
have been lording it inside your palace,
wooing your godlike wife and offering her
their marriage gifts. She longs for your return.   130
Although her heart is sad, she feeds their hopes,   [380]
by giving each man words of reassurance.
But her mind is full of other matters."

Resourceful Odysseus then answered her and said:

"Goddess, if you had not told me all this,
I would have shared the fate of Agamemnon,
son of Atreus, and died in my own home.
Come, weave a plan so I can pay them back.
Stand in person by my side, and fill me
with indomitable courage, as you did   140
when we loosed the bright diadem of Troy."

Bright-eyed goddess Athena then answered him:

"You can be sure I'll stand beside you.
I won't forget you when the trouble starts.
I think the brains and blood of many suitors
who consume your livelihood will spatter
the wide earth. But come, I'll transform you,
so you'll be unrecognizable to all.
I'll wrinkle the fine skin on your supple limbs,

remove the dark hair on your head, and then   150
dress you in rags which would make you shudder   [400]
to see clothing anyone. And your eyes,
so striking up to now, I'll make them dim.
To all those suitors you'll appear disgusting,
and to the wife and son you left at home.
You must go first of all to see the swineherd,
who tends your pigs. He's well disposed to you
and loves your son and wise Penelope.
And ask him questions about everything.
I'll go to Sparta, land of lovely women,   160
and there, Odysseus, I'll summon back
your dear son, Telemachus, who has gone
to spacious Lacedaemon, to the home
of Menelaus, to find out news of you,
to learn if you are still alive somewhere."

As she said this, Athena touched him with her staff.
She wrinkled the fair skin on his supple limbs   [430]
and took the dark hair from his head. His arms and legs
she covered with an old man's ancient flesh and dimmed
his eyes, which had been so beautiful before.   170
She dressed him in different clothes—a ragged cloak,
a dirty tunic, ripped and dishevelled, stained
with stinking smoke. Then she threw around him
a large hairless hide from a swift deer and gave him
a staff and a tattered leather pouch, full of holes
and with a twisted strap.

              When the two of them
had made their plans, they parted, and Athena went
to Lacedaemon to bring back Odysseus' son.   [440]

BOOK FOURTEEN

XIV
ODYSSEUS MEETS EUMAEUS

Odysseus left the harbour, taking the rough path
into the woods and across the hills, to the place
where Athena told him he would meet the swineherd,
who was, of all the servants lord Odysseus had,
the one who took best care of his possessions.
He found him sitting in the front part of his house,
a built-up courtyard with a panoramic view,
a large, fine place, with cleared land all around.
The swineherd built it by himself to house the pigs,
property belonging to his absent master.   10
All of a sudden the dogs observed Odysseus.
They howled and ran at him, barking furiously.   [30]
Odysseus was alert enough to drop his staff
and sit. Still, he'd have been severely mauled
in his own farmyard, but the swineherd ran up fast
behind them, dropping the leather in his hands.
Charging through the gate and shouting at his dogs,
he scattered them in a hail of stones here and there.
Then he spoke out to his master:

                              "Old man,
    those dogs would have ripped at you in no time,   20
    and then you'd have heaped the blame on me.
    Well, I've got other troubles from the gods,
    things to grieve about. For as I stay here,
    raising fat pigs for other men to eat,
    I'm full of sorrow for my noble master,   [40]
    who's probably going hungry somewhere,
    as he wanders through the lands and cities
    where men speak a foreign tongue, if, in fact,
    he's still alive and looking at the sunlight.
    But follow me, old man. Come in the hut.   30
    When you've had enough to eat and drink
    and your heart's satisfied, you can tell me
    where you come from, what troubles you've endured."

With these words, the loyal swineherd went inside the hut,
brought Odysseus in, and invited him to sit.
Odysseus was glad to get this hospitality,
so he addressed him, saying:

"Stranger,
may Zeus and other gods who live forever
give you what you truly want—you've welcomed me
with such an open heart."

Then, swineherd Eumaeus,   40
you answered him and said:[1]

"It would be wrong,
stranger, for me to disrespect a guest,
even if one worse off than you arrived,
for all guests and beggars come from Zeus."

*[Eumaeus and Odysseus talk at length. Odysseus gives a long, false
story about how he is from Crete and about how he reached Ithaca.]*

As these two were talking like this to each other,
the other herdsmen came in with their swine.   [410]
They shut the sows up in their customary pens,
so they could sleep. The pigs gave out amazing squeals,
as they were herded in. Then the trusty swineherd
called out to his companions:

"Bring a boar in here,   50
the best there is, so I can butcher it
for this stranger from another country.
We too will get some benefit from it,
seeing that we've worked hard for such a long time
and gone through troubles for these white-tusked pigs,
while others gorge themselves on our hard work
without paying anything."

Once he'd said this,
with his sharp bronze axe he chopped up wood for kindling,
while others led in a big fat boar, five years old,
and stood him by the hearth. The swineherd's heart was sound,   60   [420]
and he did not forget the gods. So he began
by throwing in the fire some bristles from the head
of the white-tusked boar and praying to all the gods
that wise Odysseus would come back to his own home.
So resourceful Odysseus spoke to him and said:

---

[1]Here the narrator makes an unexpected shift and addresses one of the characters
in person ("you"), suggesting a certain closeness between the narrator and the
character. While this is not common in Homer, it does occur several times (e.g.,
with Menelaus in the *Iliad*).

"Eumaeus, may father Zeus treat you as well [440]
as you are treating me with this boar's chine,
the very finest cut of meat, even though
I'm just a beggar."

        Then, swineherd Eumaeus,
you replied by saying:

        "Eat up, god-guided stranger, 70
and enjoy the kind of food we offer.
A god gives some things and holds others back,
as his heart prompts, for he can do all things."

Eumaeus spoke and offered to eternal gods
the first pieces he had cut. He poured gleaming wine
as a libation, passed it over to Odysseus,
sacker of cities, then sat to eat his portion.
Night came on, bringing storms. There was no moon.
And Zeus sent blustery West Wind blowing in with rain.
Eumaeus then jumped up and placed a bed 80
for Odysseus near the fire. On the bed he threw
some skins from sheep and goats. Odysseus lay down there. [520]
Eumaeus covered him with a huge thick cloak,
which he kept there as a change of clothing,
something to wear whenever a great storm blew.
So Odysseus went to sleep there, and the young men
slept around him. But Eumaeus had no wish
to have his bed inside and sleep so far away
from all his boars. So he prepared to go outside.
Odysseus was pleased he took so many troubles 90
with his master's goods while he was far away.
First, Eumaeus slung his sharp sword from his shoulder
and wrapped a really thick cloak all around him,
to keep out the wind. Then he took a massive fleece [530]
from a well-fed goat and grabbed a pointed spear
to fight off dogs and men. Then he left the hut,
going to lie down and rest where the white-tusked boars slept,
underneath a hollow rock, sheltered from North Wind.

BOOK FIFTEEN

XV

TELEMACHUS RETURNS TO ITHACA

[Pallas Athena visits Telemachus in Sparta and tells him to return home and to visit the swineherd Eumeaus. She tells him about the suitors lying in wait in an ambush. Telemachus says farewell to Menelaus and Helen and returns to Pylos, where he goes on board his ship.]

Meanwhile, Telemachus, summoned by Athena
had left Sparta for Pylos and set sail for home.
As Telemachus' comrades were approaching land,
they furled the sail and quickly lowered the mast.
Then, with their oars they rowed into an anchorage,
tossed out mooring stones, and lashed the cables at the stern.
They themselves then disembarked in the crashing surf,
to prepare a meal and mix the gleaming wine.   [500]
When they'd had food and drink to their heart's content,
prudent Telemachus was the first to speak: 10

"You men row the black ship to the city,
while I check on the fields and herdsmen.
I'll come to the city in the evening,
after I've looked over my estates.
In the morning I'll lay out a banquet
as payment to you for the journey,
a splendid meal of meat and sweetened wine."

Telemachus tied sturdy sandals on his feet,   [550]
then from the deck picked up his powerful spear
with a sharp bronze point. The crew untied stern cables   20
and then pushed out to sea, sailing to the city,
as Telemachus, godlike Odysseus' dear son,
had ordered them to do, while he strode quickly off,
his feet carrying him onward, until he reached
the farmyard and the pigs in countless numbers,
among whom the worthy swineherd lay asleep,
always thinking gentle thoughts about his master.

XVI

ODYSSEUS REVEALS HIMSELF TO TELEMACHUS

Meanwhile at dawn Odysseus and the loyal swineherd,
once they'd sent the herdsmen out with droves of pigs,
made a fire in the hut and prepared their breakfast.
As Telemachus came closer, the yelping dogs
stopped barking and fawned around him. Lord Odysseus
noticed what the dogs were doing and heard his footsteps.
At once he spoke out to Eumaeus—his words had wings:

> "Eumaeus, some comrade of yours is coming,
> or someone else you know. The dogs aren't barking
> and are acting friendly. I hear footsteps."   10

He'd hardly finished speaking when his own dear son
stood in the doorway. The swineherd, amazed, jumped up—
the bowls he was using to mix the gleaming wine
fell from his hands. He went up to greet his master,
kissed his head, both his handsome eyes, his two hands,
Then through his tears he spoke winged words to him:

> "You've come, Telemachus, you sweet light.
> I thought I'd never see you any more,
> once you went off in that ship to Pylos.
> Come in at once, dear boy, so that my heart   20
> can rejoice to see you here in my home,
> now you've just returned from distant places."

Once he'd said this, he took Telemachus' bronze spear   [40]
and let him enter. He crossed the stone threshold.
As he approached, Odysseus, his father, got up
to offer him his seat, but from across the room
Telemachus stopped him and said:

>   "Stay put, stranger.
> We'll find a chair in the hut somewhere else.
> Here's a man who will get one for us."

He spoke. Odysseus went back and sat down again.   30
Eumaeus piled up green brushwood on the floor
and spread a fleece on top. Odysseus' dear son
sat down there. The swineherd then set out before them
platters of roast meat, left over from the meal   [50]
they'd had the day before, and quickly heaped up
baskets full of bread. In a wooden bowl he mixed

wine sweet as honey, and then sat down himself,
opposite godlike Odysseus. Their hands reached out
to the fine meal prepared and spread before them.
When they'd had food and drink to their heart's content,   40
Telemachus then said to the splendid swineherd:

> "Old friend, you must go quickly and report   [130]
> to wise Penelope that I've returned,
> I'm safely home from Pylos. I'll stay here,
> until you've given the news to her alone
> and come back here. No other Achaean
> must learn about it, for many of them
> are planning nasty things against me.
> But after you've delivered your message,   [150]
> then come back here. Don't go wandering   50
> around the fields looking for Laertes.
> Instead, tell my mother to send her maid,
> the housekeeper, quickly and in secret.
> She can report the news to the old man."

His words spurred on the swineherd. He took his sandals,
tied them on his feet, and set off for the city.

Now, it did not escape the notice of Athena
that swineherd Eumaeus was going from the farm.
She approached the hut, appearing like a woman,
beautiful, tall, and skilled in making lovely things.   60
She stood just outside the entrance to the farm
and was visible to no one but Odysseus.
Telemachus did not see her face to face   [160]
or notice she was there. For when gods appear,
there's no way their form is perceptible to all.
But Odysseus saw her. So did the dogs, as well.
But they didn't bark. Instead, they crept away,
whimpering in fear, to the far side of the hut.
She signalled with her eyebrows. Lord Odysseus
noticed and went out of the hut, past the large wall   70
around the yard, and stood in front of her.
Then Athena spoke to him:

> "Son of Laertes,
> resourceful Odysseus, sprung from Zeus,
> Now is the time to speak to your own son—
> make yourself known and don't conceal the facts,
> so you two can plan the suitors' lethal fate,

then go together to the famous city.   [170]
I won't be absent from you very long—
I'm eager for the battle."

                         As she said this, Athena
touched Odysseus with her golden wand. To start with,   80
she placed a well-washed cloak around his body,
then made him taller and restored his youthful looks.
His skin grew dark once more, his countenance filled out,
and the beard around his chin turned black again.
Once she'd done this, Athena left. But Odysseus
returned into the hut. His dear son was amazed.
He turned his eyes away, afraid it was a god,
and spoke to him—his words had wings: [180]

                             "Stranger,
you look different to me than you did before—
you're wearing different clothes, your skin has changed.   90
You're one of the gods who hold wide heaven.
If so, be gracious, so we can give you
pleasing offerings, well-crafted gifts of gold.
But spare us."

                         Long-suffering lord Odysseus
then answered him and said:

                    "I'm not one of the gods.
Why do you compare me to immortals?
But I am your father, on whose account
you grieve and suffer so much trouble,
having to endure men's acts of violence."

Once he'd said this, he sat down, and Telemachus   100
embraced his noble father, cried out, and shed tears.
A desire to lament arose in both of them—
they wailed aloud, as insistently as birds,
like sea eagles or hawks with curving talons
whose young have been carried off by country folk
before they're fully fledged. That's how both men then
let tears of pity fall from underneath their eyelids.
And now light from the sun would have gone down on them,   [220]
as they wept, if Telemachus had not spoken.
He suddenly addressed his father:

                    "In what kind of ship,   110
dear father, did sailors bring you here,

to Ithaca? Who did they say they were?
For I don't think you made it here on foot."

Noble long-suffering Odysseus answered him:

"All right, my child, I'll tell you the truth.
Phaeacians, those famous sailors, brought me.
They escort other men, as well, all those
who visit them. But come now, tell me
about the number of the suitors,
so I know how many men there are   120
and what they're like. Then, once my noble heart
has thought it over, I'll make up my mind,
whether we two are powerful enough
to take them on alone, without assistance,
or whether we should seek out other men."

Shrewd Telemachus answered him and said: [240]

                           "Father,
I've always heard about your great renown,
a mighty warrior—your hands are very strong,
your plans intelligent. But what you say
is far too big a task. I'm astonished.   130
Two men cannot fight against so many,
and they are powerful. In an exact count,
there are not just ten suitors or twice ten,
but many more. Here, you can soon add up
their numbers—from Dulichium there are
fifty-two hand-picked young men, six servants
in their retinue, from Same twenty-four,
from Zacynthus twenty young Achaeans,   [250]
and from Ithaca itself twelve young men,
all nobility. Medon, the herald,   140
is with them, as is the godlike minstrel,
and two attendants skilled in carving meat.
If we move against all these men inside,
I fear revenge may bring a bitter fate,
now you've come home. So you should consider
whether you can think of anyone who'll help,
someone prepared to stand by both of us
and fight with all his heart."

                           Then lord Odysseus,
who had endured so much, answered him and said:

"All right, I'll tell you. Pay attention now,   150
and listen. Do you believe Athena,   [260]
along with Father Zeus, will be enough
for the two of us, or should I think about
someone else to help us?"

                 Shrewd Telemachus
then said in reply:

        "Those two allies you mention
are excellent. They sit high in the clouds,
ruling others, men and immortal gods."

Long-suffering lord Odysseus answered him and said:

"The two of them won't stand apart for long
from the great fight—we can be sure of that—   160
when Ares' warlike spirit in my halls
is put to the test between these suitors
and ourselves. But for now, when Dawn arrives,   [270]
go to the house, join those arrogant suitors.
The swineherd will bring me to the city
later on. I'll be looking like a beggar,
old and wretched. If they're abusive to me,
let that dear heart in your chest endure it,
while I'm being badly treated, even if
they drag me by my feet throughout the house   170
and out the door or throw things and hit me.
Keep looking on, and hold yourself in check.
You can tell them to stop their foolishness,
but seek to win them over with nice words,
even though you'll surely not convince them,
because the day they meet their fate has come.   [280]
I'll tell you something else—keep it in mind.
When wise Athena puts it in my mind,
I'll nod my head to you. When you see that,
take all the weapons of war lying there,   180
in the hall, and put them in a secret place,
all of them, in the lofty storage room.
But leave behind a pair of swords, two spears,
and two ox-hide shields, for the two of us
to grab up when we make a rush at them,
while Pallas Athena and Counsellor Zeus
will keep the suitors' minds preoccupied.
I'll tell you something else—keep it in mind.

If you are my son and truly of our blood,   [300]
let no one hear Odysseus is back home.   190
Don't let Laertes know or the swineherd,
or any servants, or Penelope herself."

So the two men talked about these things together.

Meanwhile, the well-built ship which brought Telemachus
from Pylos with all his comrades had reached Ithaca.
Once they'd come inside the deep water harbour,
they hauled the black ship up on shore. Eager servants
carried off their weapons and without delay
took the splendid gifts to Clytius' home.
They also sent a herald to Odysseus' house,   200
to report to wise Penelope, telling her
Telemachus had gone to visit the estates   [330]
and had told the ship to sail off for the city,
in case the noble queen might get sick at heart
and shed some tears. This herald and the swineherd met
because they'd both been sent off with the same report
to tell the queen. When they reached the royal palace,
the herald spoke out in front of female servants:

"My queen, your dear son has just returned."

But the swineherd came up close to Penelope   210
and gave her all the details her dear son
had ordered him to say. Once he'd told her   [340]
every item he'd been asked to mention to her,
he went off, leaving the courtyard and the hall,
back to his pigs. The suitors were unhappy,
their hearts dismayed, and they departed from the hall,
past the large courtyard wall. There, before the gates,
they sat down. The first one of them to say something
was Eurymachus, son of Polybus:

"O my friends,
to tell the truth, in his great arrogance   220
Telemachus has carried out his trip,
a huge achievement. We never thought
he would complete it. So come on now,
let's launch a black ship, the best one we have,
collect some sailors, a crew of rowers,

so they can quickly carry a report
to those other men to go home at once."[1]   [350]

No sooner had he said all this, than Amphinomus,
turning in his place, saw a ship in the deep harbour.
Men were bringing down the sail, others holding oars.   230
With a hearty laugh, he then addressed his comrades:

"Don't bother with a message any more.
Here they are back home. Either some god
gave them news, or they saw his ship themselves,
as it sailed past, but couldn't catch it."

He spoke. They all got up and went to the sea shore,
then quickly dragged the black ship up onto dry ground,
while eager attendants carried off their weapons.   [360]
They themselves went to the meeting place together.
No one else was allowed to sit there with them,   240
no old or younger men. Then Antinous addressed them,
son of Eupeithes:

                    "Well, this is bad news—
the gods have delivered the man from harm.
Our lookouts sat each day on windy heights,
always in successive shifts. At sunset,
we never spent the night on shore, but sailed
over the sea in our swift ship, waiting
for sacred Dawn, as we set our ambush
for Telemachus, so we could capture
and then kill him. Meanwhile, some god   250 [370]
has brought him home. But let's think about
a sad end for Telemachus right here
and ensure he doesn't get away from us.
For as long as he's alive, I don't think
we'll be successful in what we're doing.
He himself is clever, shrewd in counsel,
and now people don't regard us well at all.
So come now, before he calls Achaeans
to assembly. I don't think he will give up.
He'll get angry and stand up to proclaim   260
to everyone how we planned to kill him
and how we didn't get him. The people

[1]The "other men" are the ones waiting in the islands to ambush Telemachus.

109

will resent us, once they learn about   [380]
our nasty acts. Take care they do not harm us
and force us out, away from our own land,
until we reach a foreign country. And so,
let's move first—capture him out in the fields,
far from the city, or else on the road.
If what I've been saying displeases you,
and you'd prefer he should remain alive,   270
retaining all the riches of his fathers,
then let's not keep on gathering in this place,
consuming his supply of pleasant things.
Instead, let each man carry on his courtship   [390]
from his own home, seeking to prevail with gifts.
Then she can marry the one who offers most
and comes to her as her destined husband."

He finished. They all sat quiet, not saying a thing.
Then Amphinomus spoke out and addressed them,
splendid son of lord Nisus. With good intentions,   280
he spoke to them and said:

                    "My friends,   [400]
I wouldn't want to slay Telemachus.
It's reprehensible to kill someone
of royal blood. But first let's ask the gods
for their advice. If great Zeus' oracles
approve the act, I myself will kill him
and tell all other men to do so, too.
But if the gods decline, I say we stop."

Amphinomus finished. They agreed with what he'd said.
So they immediately got up and went away   290
to Odysseus' house. Once they reached the palace,
they sat down on the polished chairs in the great hall.

At evening the fine swineherd came to Odysseus
and to his son, busy getting dinner ready.
They'd killed a boar, one year old. Then Athena
approached Odysseus, Laertes' son, and touched him
with her wand and made him an old man once again.
She put shabby clothes around his body, just in case
the swineherd, by looking up, would recognize him
and then go off to tell faithful Penelope,   300
and thus fail to keep the secret in his heart.

XVII
ODYSSEUS GOES TO THE PALACE AS A BEGGAR

As soon as rose-fingered early Dawn appeared,
Telemachus, dear son of god-like Odysseus,
tied some fine sandals on his feet, took a strong spear,
well suited to his grip, and, as he headed off
towards the city, spoke out to the swineherd:

"Old friend, I'm leaving for the city,
so my mother can observe me. I don't think
her dreadful grieving and her sorry tears
will stop until she sees me for herself.
So I'm telling you to do as follows—   10
take this wretched stranger to the city.   [10]
Once there, he can beg food from anyone
who'll offer him some bread and cups of water.
I can't take on the weight of everyone,
not when I have these sorrows in my heart.
As for the stranger, if he's very angry,
things will be worse for him. Those are the facts,
and I do like to speak the truth."

                                              Odysseus,
that resourceful man, then answered him and said:

"Friend, I myself am not all that eager   20
to be held back here. For a beggar man
it's better to ask people for a meal
in the city instead of in the fields.
Whoever's willing will give me something."

Odysseus finished. Telemachus walked away,
across the farmyard, moving with rapid strides.
He was sowing seeds of trouble for the suitors.
When he entered the beautifully furnished house,
Telemachus walked through the hall, gripping his spear.
Two swift dogs went with him. The arrogant suitors   30
thronged around him, making gentle conversation,
but deep in their hearts they were planning trouble.

*[Telemachus has a brief reunion with his mother, Penelope. A meal
is prepared in the hall and they sit down.]*

Telemachus' mother sat across from him,
by the door post of the hall, leaning from her seat

to spin fine threads of yarn. They stretched out their hands
to take the fine food prepared and set before them.
When they'd had food and drink to their heart's content,
the first to speak to them was wise Penelope: [100]

>"Telemachus, once I've gone up to my room,
>I'll lie down in bed, which has become for me   40
>a place where I lament, always wet with tears,
>ever since Odysseus went to Troy
>with Atreus' sons. Yet you don't dare
>to tell me clearly of your father's trip,
>even before the haughty suitors come
>into the house, no word of what you learned."

Shrewd Telemachus then answered her and said:

>"All right then, mother, I'll tell you the truth.
>We went to Pylos and reached Nestor,
>shepherd of his people. He welcomed us   50   [110]
>in his lofty home with hospitality
>and kindness, as a father for a son
>who's just returned from far-off places
>after many years—that's how Nestor
>and his splendid sons looked after me
>with loving care. But of brave Odysseus,
>alive or dead, he told me he'd heard nothing
>from any man on earth. He sent me off
>with horses and a well-built chariot
>to that famous spearman Menelaus,   60
>son of Atreus. There I saw Argive Helen,
>for whom many Trojans and Achaeans
>struggled hard, because that's what gods had willed.
>Menelaus, skilled at war shouts, at once   [120]
>asked me why I'd come to lovely Sparta,
>what I was looking for. I told him the truth,
>all the details. He answered me and said:

>>'That's disgraceful! They want to lie down
>>in the bed of a courageous warrior,
>>when they themselves are cowards—just as if   70
>>a doe has put two new-born suckling fawns
>>in a mighty lion's thicket, so they can sleep,
>>and roams mountain slopes and grassy valleys
>>seeking pasture, and then the lion comes
>>back to that lair and brings a dismal fate   [130]

for both of them—that's how Odysseus
will bring those men to their disastrous end.'

"That's what famous spearman Menelaus said,
the son of Atreus. When I was finished,
I came home, and the immortals gave me   80
favourable winds which quickly carried me
back to my native land."

            Meanwhile Odysseus
and the loyal swineherd were hastening to leave,
moving from the fields into the city.
Eumaeus gave him a staff he liked, and then
the two of them set off. The dogs and herdsmen   [200]
stayed behind to guard the farmyard. The swineherd
led his master to the city, like a beggar,
leaning on a stick, an old and miserable man,
with his body wrapped in wretched clothing.   90
But as they walked along the rugged pathway,
getting near the city, they reached a well-made spring,
with a steady flow, where townsfolk drew their water,
Here Melanthius, son of Dolius, met them—
he was driving on some goats, the finest ones
in all the herds, to serve as dinner for the suitors.
Two herdsmen followed with him. When he saw them,
Melanthius started yelling insults. What he said
was shameful and abusive—it stirred Odysseus' heart.

"Now here we have a truly filthy man   100
leading on another filthy scoundrel.
As always, god matches like with like.
You miserable swineherd, where are you going
with this disgusting pig, this beggar man,
a tedious bore who'll interrupt our feasts?   [220]

Melanthius finished, and as he moved on past them,
in his stupidity he kicked Odysseus on the hip,
then left them there, as they walked slowly onward.
He strode ahead and quickly reached the royal palace.
He went in at once and sat among the suitors,   110
opposite Eurymachus, who was fond of him
more than the others were. Those serving at the meal
laid down a portion of the meat in front of him.
The respected housekeeper brought in the bread
and placed it there for him to eat.

Meanwhile Odysseus   [260]
and the loyal swineherd paused as they came closer.
Around them rang the music of the hollow lyre,
for Phemius was striking up a song to sing.

[Odysseus and Eumaeus decide to enter the hall separately]

As the swineherd Eumaeus came inside the house,
godlike Telemachus was the first to see him,   120
well before the others. He quickly summoned him
by nodding. Eumaeus looked around, then picked up   [330]
a stool lying where a servant usually sat
to carve large amounts of meat to serve the suitors,
when they feasted in the house. He took this stool,
placed it by Telemachus' table, facing him,
and then sat down. Meanwhile, a herald brought him
a portion of the meat, set it in front of him,
and lifted some bread for him out of the basket.
Odysseus came into the house behind Eumaeus,   130
looking like an old and miserable beggar,
leaning on his staff, his body dressed in rags.
He sat on the ash wood threshold in the doorway,
propping his back against a post of cypress wood,
which a craftsman had once planed with skill   [340]
and set in true alignment. Then the goatherd,
Melanthius, spoke out to them:

                    "Listen to me,   [370]
those of you courting the glorious queen,
about this stranger. I've seen him before.
The swineherd was the one who brought him here.   140
I don't know his identity for sure
or the family he claims to come from."

Once he'd said this, Antinous turned on Eumaeus,
to reprimand him:

                    "You really are a man
who cares for pigs—why bring this fellow here
into the city? As far as vagrants go,
don't we have enough apart from him,
greedy beggars who disrupt our banquets?
Do you think too few of them come here
and waste away your master's livelihood,   150
so you invite this man to come as well?"

Then, swineherd Eumaeus, you answered him and said: [380]

"Antinous, you may be a noble man,
but what you've said is not a worthy speech.
You are abusive to Odysseus' slaves,
more so than any of the other suitors,
especially to me. But I don't care,
not while faithful Penelope lives here,   [390]
in these halls, and godlike Telemachus."

[Odysseus moves around begging food from the suitors]

Then Antinous spoke out and said:

                         "What god   160
sent this nuisance to interrupt our feast?
You're an insolent and shameless beggar—
you come up to every man, one by one,
and they give you things without holding back,   [450]
for there's no check or scruple when one gives
from someone else's goods, and each of them
has plenty of supplies in front of him."

Resourceful Odysseus then moved back and replied:

"Well now, it seems as if that mind of yours
doesn't match your looks—you'd refuse to give   170
even a grain of salt from your own house
to a follower of yours, and now you sit
in someone else's house and do not dare
to take some bread and offer it to me.
And yet there's plenty right in front of you."

Odysseus finished. Antinous in his heart
was even angrier than before. He glared at him,
then, with a scowl, replied—his words had wings:

"I no longer think you'll leave this hall unharmed,   [460]
now that you've begun to babble insults."   180

As he said this, he grabbed a stool and threw it.
It hit the bottom of Odysseus' right shoulder,
where it joins the back. But he stood firm, like a rock—
what Antinous had thrown did not make him stagger.
He shook his head in silence, making cruel plans,
then went back to the door and sat down there.

Meanwhile, Penelope talked with her serving women,
sitting in her room, while lord Odysseus ate.
Then she called out to the loyal swineherd, saying:

"Good Eumaeus, go and ask the stranger   190
to come here, so I can greet him warmly
and ask if he perhaps has heard about   [510]
my brave Odysseus, or caught sight of him
with his own eyes. He looks like a man
who's spent a long time wandering around."

Penelope finished. Once Eumaeus heard her,
he went off and, standing beside Odysseus,
spoke to him—his words had wings:

                    "Honoured stranger,
wise Penelope is summoning you,
Telemachus' mother. For her heart,   200
in spite of bearing much anxiety,
is telling her to ask about her husband."

Odysseus then answered him: [560]

          "Eumaeus, I'll tell the truth,
all the details, to wise Penelope,
daughter of Icarius, and quickly, too.
For I know Odysseus well. Tell Penelope,
for all her eagerness, to wait right now,
there in the hall, until the sun goes down.   [570]
Let her ask me then about her husband
and the day of his return. And let me sit   210
close to the fire, for the clothes I have
are pitiful, as you know for yourself,
since I came to you first of all for help."

[Eumaeus tells Penelope what Odysseus has said.]

The loyal swineherd joined the crowd of suitors.   [590]
He quickly spoke winged words to Telemachus,
holding his head close to him, so others could not hear:

"Friend, I'm going to leave and guard the swine
and other things, your livelihood and mine.
You take charge of all the problems here.
First and foremost, protect yourself. Your heart   220
must stay alert, so you don't suffer harm."

Shrewd Telemachus then answered him and said:

"It will happen, old friend. Now, you should eat
before you leave. Come here in the morning,
and bring fine animals for sacrifice.   [600]
Everything going on here is my concern,
mine and the immortals."

                                        Telemachus spoke.
The swineherd sat down on the polished chair again.
Once he'd filled his heart with food and drink, he left,
returning to his pigs, through the courtyard and the hall   230
full of banqueters, who were enjoying themselves
with dance and song, for evening had already come.

Book Nineteen

XVIII
Odysseus and Irus the Beggar

[Irus, a beggar who helps out the suitors, arrives at the palace and starts abusing Odysseus; they fight, and Odysseus knocks Irus out; Penelope encourages the suitors to bring presents for her, and they do so; Odysseus talks to the female servants, criticizing them for assisting the suitors; Eurymachus makes fun of Odysseus and throws a stool at him but misses and hits the wine steward; the suitors continue feasting and then leave]

XIX
Eurycleia Recognizes Odysseus

[Telemachus and Odysseus remove the weapons from the hall and conceal them in a storage room.]

Telemachus moved off, going through the hall,
below the flaming torches, out into the room
where he used to rest when sweet sleep came to him.
Then he lay down there and waited for the dawn.
Lord Odysseus remained behind, in the hall,   [50]
thinking how to kill the suitors with Athena's help.
Then wise Penelope emerged out of her room,
looking like Artemis or golden Aphrodite.
Beside the fire where she used to sit, they placed
a chair for her, inlaid with ivory and silver.   10
Here wise Penelope sat, then spoke to Eurynome,
her housekeeper, and said:

            "Eurynome,
bring a chair over here with a fleece on it,
so the stranger can sit down and talk to me
and hear me out. I want to question him."

Once Penelope had spoken, Eurynome   [100]
quickly brought a polished chair and placed it there.
She threw a sheep fleece over it. Lord Odysseus,
who had endured so much, sat down on it. And then
wise Penelope began their conversation: 20

    "Stranger, first of all I'll ask this question—
Who are you among men? Where are you from?
From what city? And where are your parents?"

Resourceful Odysseus then answered her:

118

"Noble lady,
wife of Odysseus, all right, I'll tell you.
But you will be giving me more sorrows
than those which grip me here—as is the rule
when a man's been absent from his native land
as long as I have now, wandering around,   [170]
through many towns of mortal men, suffering   30
great distress. Still, I'll answer what you ask,
the questions you have posed. There's a place
in the middle of the wine-dark sea called Crete,
where I was born, son of king Deucalion,
son of Minos. I saw Odysseus there
and gave him welcoming gifts. The wind's force
brought him to Crete, as he was sailing on,
bound for Troy. So I invited him
into my house and entertained him well,
with a kind welcome, using the rich store   40
of goods inside my house."

                    As Odysseus spoke,
he made the many falsehood seem like truth.
Penelope listened with tears flowing down.
Her flesh melted—just as on high mountains
snow melts away under West Wind's thaw,
once East Wind blows it down, and, as it melts,
the flowing rivers fill—that's how her fair cheeks
melted then, as she shed tears for her husband,
who was sitting there beside her. Odysseus
felt pity in his heart for his grieving wife,   50   [210]
but his eyes stayed firm between his eyelids,
like horn or iron, and he kept up his deceit
to conceal his tears. But then, when Penelope
had had enough of crying and mourning,
she spoke to him once more and said:

                    "Now, stranger,
I think I'd really like to test you out,
to see if you did, in fact, entertain
my husband and his fine companions there,
in your halls, as you just claimed. So tell me
what sort of clothes he had on his body   60
and the kind of man he was. And tell me
about his comrades who went there with him."

Resourceful Odysseus then answered her and said: [220]

> "Lady, it's difficult to tell you this
> for any man who's been away so long—
> it's now the twentieth year since he went off
> and left my country. But I'll describe for you
> how my heart pictures him. Lord Odysseus
> wore a woollen purple cloak, a double one.
> The brooch on it was made of gold—it had   70
> a pair of clasps and a fine engraving
> on the front, a dog clutched in its forepaws
> a dappled fawn, gripping it as it writhed.
> Everyone who saw it was astonished
> at those gold animals—the dog held down   [230]
> the fawn, as he throttled it, and the fawn
> was struggling with its feet, trying to flee.
> I noticed the tunic on his body—
> glistening like the skin of a dry onion—
> it was so soft and shone out like the sun."   80

As Odysseus spoke, in Penelope he roused
desire to weep still more, because she recognized
in what Odysseus said signs that he spoke the truth.   [250]
But then, when she'd had enough of tearful sorrow,
she answered him and said these words:

>   "Stranger,
> though I pitied you before, in my home
> you'll now find genuine welcome and respect.
> I was the one who gave him that clothing
> you talk about. I brought it from the room,
> folded it, and pinned on the shining brooch   90
> to be an ornament for him. But now,
> I'll not be welcoming him here again,
> when he returns to his dear native land."   [260]

Resourceful Odysseus then answered her and said:

> "Noble wife of Odysseus, Laertes' son,
> don't mar your lovely skin or waste your heart
> by weeping for your husband. End your crying,
> and listen to my words. I'll tell you the truth,
> hiding nothing—for I've already heard   [270]
> about Odysseus' return. He's close by,   100

in the wealthy land of Thesprotians,
still alive and bringing much fine treasure."

Wise Penelope then answered him:

       "O stranger,
I wish what you have said might come about.
You'd soon come to recognize my friendship,   [310]
so many gifts from me that any man
who met you would call you truly blessed.
But my heart has a sense of what will be—
Odysseus won't be coming home again,
and you'll not find a convoy out of here,   110
because there are no leaders in this house,
not the quality of man Odysseus was.
But, you servant women, wash this stranger,
and prepare a place to sleep—a bed, cloaks,
bright coverlets—so in warmth and comfort
he may reach Dawn with her golden throne."

Resourceful Odysseus then answered her and said:

"Honoured wife of Odysseus, Laertes' son,
I've hated cloaks and shining coverlets
since I first left the mountain snows of Crete,   120
when I departed on my long-oared ship.
So I'll lie down, as I've been doing before   [340]
through sleepless nights. I've lain many nights
on foul bedding, awaiting bright-throned Dawn.
And having my feet washed brings no delight
into my heart. No woman in your household
will touch my feet, none of the serving women
in your home, unless there is an old one,
who knows true devotion and has suffered
in her heart as many pains as I have.   130
I'd not resent it if she touched my feet."

Wise Penelope then answered him and said:

"Dear stranger, no guest from distant lands   [350]
who's come into my house has ever been
as wise as you or more welcome—your words
are all so sensible and thoughtful. I do have
an old woman with an understanding heart.
She gave my helpless husband her fine care
the day his mother first gave birth to him.

Although she's weak and old, she'll wash your feet.   140
So come now, stand up, wise Eurycleia,
and bathe a man the same age as your master."

Penelope spoke, and the old woman held her hands
over her face and shed warm tears. She spoke out
uttering words of sorrow:

                    "And I'm willing.
So for Penelope's sake I'll bathe your feet."

The old woman took the shining bowl to wash his feet.
She poured in plenty of cold water and added
warmer water to it. Odysseus then sat down
some distance from the hearth and quickly turned around   150
towards the darkness. For suddenly in his heart
he was afraid that, when she touched him, she might see   [390]
a scar he had, and then the truth would be revealed.
She came up and began to wash her master.
She recognized the scar immediately, a wound
a boar's white tusk had given him many years ago,
when he'd gone to Parnassus, making a visit
to Autolycus, his mother's splendid father.
She traced it out and recognized it. She dropped his foot.
His leg fell in the basin, and the bronze rang out.   160
It tipped onto its side. Water spilled out on the ground.   [470]
All at once, joy and sorrow gripped her heart. Her eyes
filled up with tears, and her full voice was speechless.
She reached up to his chin and said:

                    "It's true, dear child.
You are Odysseus, and I didn't know you,
not till I'd touched all my master's body."

She spoke, and her eyes glanced over at Penelope,
anxious to tell her that her husband had come home.
Then Odysseus' arms reached out for Eurycleia—
with his right hand he grabbed her by the throat,   170 [480]
and with the other pulled her closer to him.
Then he said:

                    "My good mother, why this wish
to have me slaughtered? You yourself nursed me
at this breast of yours. Now in the twentieth year,
after suffering through numerous ordeals,
I've come back to my native land. And now,

you've recognized me—a god has put that
in your heart. Stay silent, so in these halls
no one else finds out. I'll tell you something—
and it will happen. If a god overpowers   180
these arrogant suitors, sets them under me,
I'll not spare you, though you are my nurse,
when I kill other women in my home."   [490]

Once Odysseus spoke, the old woman left the room
to fetch water for his feet, since what she'd had before
had all been spilled. When she'd finished bathing him,
she rubbed him with rich oil. Then Odysseus once more
pulled his chair closer to the fire to warm himself.
He hid the scar under his rags. Wise Penelope
began to speak. She said:

       "Stranger, there's one small thing   190
I'll ask you for myself. Soon it will be time
to take a pleasant rest. And sleep is sweet   [510]
to anyone it seizes, even if he's troubled.
But some god has given me unmeasured grief,
for every day I get my joy from mourning,
from laments, as I look after my own work
and supervise the servants in the house.
But when night comes and Sleep grips everyone,
I lie in bed, and piercing worries crowd
my throbbing heart and give me great distress.   200
Should I stay with my son and keep careful watch
on all possessions and my female slaves
and my large and lofty home, honouring
my husband's bed and what the people say,
or go off with the best of those Achaeans
who court me in my halls—the one who offers
countless bridal gifts. My son, while young   [530]
and with a feeble mind, would not permit
that I got married and left my husband's home.
But now he's grown—his youth has reached its limit—   210
he's begging me to go back home again,
to leave this house, for he's very worried
about the property which these Achaeans
are using up. But come, listen to my dream
and interpret it for me. In this house
I have twenty geese come from the water
to eat my wheat. And when I look at them

I am delighted. Then from the mountains
a huge hook-beaked eagle came and killed them—
snapping all their necks. They lay there in piles,   220
inside my hall, while he was carried up   [540]
into a shining sky. Now in that dream
I wept and wailed. Meanwhile, all around me
fair-haired women of Achaea gathered,
as, in my sorrow, I was there lamenting
that the eagle had slaughtered all my geese.
But he came back and, sitting on a beam
projecting from the roof, checked my sorrow,
and in a human voice spoke out to me:

     'Daughter of famous Icarius,   230
     you must be brave. That was no dream,
     but a true glimpse of what will really happen.
     The suitors are those geese, and I am here—
     before I was an eagle, but now I've come
     as your own husband, who will execute
     a cruel fate on each and every suitor.'   [550]

"That's what he said. Then sweet sleep released me.
When I looked around the hall, I saw the geese—
they were pecking at the wheat beside the trough,
as they used to do before."

                    Resourceful Odysseus   240
then answered her and said:

             "Lady, it's quite impossible
to twist another meaning from this dream,
since the real Odysseus has revealed to you
how he will end all this. The suitors' deaths
are all plain to see, and not one of them
will escape destruction and his fate."

Wise Penelope then gave him her reply:

"Stranger, stories told in dreams are difficult—   [560]
their meanings are not clear, and for people
they are not realized in every detail.   250
There are two gates for insubstantial dreams,
one made of horn and one of ivory.
Those which pass through the fresh-cut ivory
deceive—the words they bring are unfulfilled.
Those which come through the gate of polished horn,

once some mortal sees them, bring on the truth.
But, in my case, I don't think that strange dream
came through that gate. It really would have been
a welcome thing to me and to my son.
But I'll tell you something else. Keep it in mind.   260 [570]
That morning is already drawing near
which will separate me from Odysseus' house,
a day of evil omen. I'll now organize
a competition featuring those axes
he used to set inside his hall, in a line,
like a ship's ribs, twelve of them in all.
He'd stand far off and shoot an arrow through them.
I'll now set up this contest for the suitors.
The one whose hand most deftly strings his bow
and shoots an arrow through all twelve axes   270
is the one I'll go with.[1] I'll leave my house,
where I've been married, a very lovely home,   [580]
full of what one needs to live—even in dreams
it will stay in my memory forever."

Resourceful Odysseus then answered her and said:

"Honoured wife of Odysseus, Laertes' son,
don't delay this contest in your halls
a moment longer. I can assure you,
Odysseus will be here with all his schemes,
before these men pick up the polished bow,   280
string it, and shoot an arrow through the iron."

Wise Penelope began to speak. She said:

                              "Stranger,
if you wished to sit beside me in these halls
to bring me pleasure, sleep would never sit   [590]
on these eyelids of mine. But there's no way
men can go on forever without sleep.
Immortal gods have set a proper time

---

[1]The details of this famous trial of shooting an arrow through a row of axes have
been much discussed. Some interpreters have suggested that it makes sense if we
imagine that there is a hole in the head of each axe and that they can be lined up
so that an arrow might pass through them all (obviously a very difficult shot).
Some ancient axes apparently had this feature. Others have suggested that the
holes are rings at the bottom end of the shaft or that the holes are those which
normally hold the axe shaft (so that the line of axes is actually a line of axe heads
with the shaft removed). There are other suggestions, too.

for every man on this grain-bearing earth.
So now I'll go up to my upper room
and lie down on the bed, which is for me   290
a place for grieving, always wet with tears,
since Odysseus went to wicked Ilion,
a name which never should be mentioned.
I'll lie down there. But you can stretch out here,
in the house, putting bedding on the floor.
Or let the servants make a bed for you."

Once she'd said this, she went to her bright upper room,   [600]
not alone, for two attendant women went with her.
When she and her servants reached the upper room,
she cried out for Odysseus, her dear husband,   300
till bright-eyed Athena cast sweet sleep on her eyelids.

BOOK TWENTY

XX

ODYSSEUS PREPARES FOR HIS REVENGE

When Dawn arrived inside Odysseus' splendid home,
women slaves were up and making tireless fire
Then the men who served Achaean lords arrived.   [160]
Behind them came the swineherd, leading in three hogs,
the best of all he had. He turned them loose to feed
inside the lovely yard, while he talked to Odysseus,
with words of reassurance:

                    "Stranger, these Achaeans—
do they have any more regard for you?
Or in these halls are they dishonouring you,
they way they did before?"

                    Shrewd Odysseus   10
then answered him and said:

                    "Well, Eumaeus,
I hope the gods pay back the injuries
arrogant men so recklessly have planned   [170]
in someone else's home, with no sense of shame."

As these two were saying these words to one another,
Melanthius, the goatherd, came up close to them,
leading the very finest she-goats in his flocks,
part of the suitors' feast. Two herdsmen came with him.
He tied the goats up by the echoing portico,
then started hurling his insults at Odysseus: 20

    "Stranger, are you still bothering us here,
    inside the house, begging from the people?
    Why don't you get out? I think it's clear   [180]
    the two of us won't say goodbye, until
    we've had a taste of one another's fists.
    The way you beg is not appropriate.
    Achaeans do have feasts in other places."

Melanthius spoke, but shrewd Odysseus said nothing.
He shook his head in silence. Deep in his heart
he was planning trouble. Then a third one joined them,   30
Philoetius, an outstanding man, bringing in
a sterile heifer and plump she-goats for the suitors.

He tied these animals with care, approached Odysseus,
and spoke to him—his words had wings:

> "Greetings, honoured stranger.
> Though you're facing many troubles now,
> may you find happiness in future days. [200]
> When I recall Odysseus and think of him,
> I start to sweat. My eyes fill up with tears.
> For he, too, I think, is dressed in rags like these,
> wandering among men somewhere, if indeed 40
> he's still alive, looking at the sunlight."

Resourceful Odysseus then answered him and said:

> "Herdsman, you don't appear to be a man
> who's bad or one who lacks intelligence.
> I see for myself your understanding heart.
> And so I'll swear a powerful oath to you.
> Odysseus will come home. With your own eyes,
> you'll see the suitors killed, if that's your wish,
> those men who act as if they own the place."

The cattle herder answered him:

> "Ah stranger, 50
> how I wish Cronos' son might bring about
> what you've just said. Then you'd find out
> how strong I am and what my hands can do."

Eumaeus also prayed like that to all the gods
for wise Odysseus' return to his own home.

[The suitors continue to feast and to abuse Odysseus in disguise.]

XXI

The Contest with Odysseus' Bow

Bright-eyed Athena then placed inside the heart
of wise Penelope, Icarius' daughter,
the thought that she should set up in Odysseus' halls
the bow and the grey iron axes for the suitors,
as a competition and the prelude to their deaths.

*[Penelope goes to the storage chamber, collects Odysseus' bow and
his axes, and returns]*

Once the lovely lady reached the suitors, she stood there,
by the door post of the well-constructed hall,
with a bright veil on her face. On either side
stood loyal attendant women. Then Penelope
addressed the suitors with these words:

       "Listen to me,   10
bold suitors, who've been ravaging this home
with your incessant need for food and drink,
since my husband's now been so long absent.   [70]
The only story you could offer up
as an excuse is that you all desire
to marry me and take me as your wife.
So come now, suitors, since I seem to be
the prize you seek, I'll place this great bow here
belonging to godlike Odysseus. And then,
whichever one of you can grip this bow   20
and string it with the greatest ease, then shoot
an arrow through twelve axes, all of them,
I'll go with him, leaving my married home,
this truly lovely house and all these goods
one needs to live—things I'll remember,
even in my dreams."

       When she'd said this,   [80]
she then told Eumaeus, the loyal swineherd,
to set the bow and grey iron axes for the suitors.
Then among them all Telemachus spoke out
with royal authority:

       "Well now, Zeus,   30
son of Cronos, must have made me foolish—
my dear mother, although quite sensible,

says she'll be leaving with another man,
abandoning this home, and I just laugh.
My witless heart finds that enjoyable."

After he'd said this, Telemachus threw off
the purple cloak covering his back, jumped up,
and removed the sharp sword from his shoulders.
First, he set up the axes. He dug a trench,   [120]
one long ditch for all of them, in a straight line.[1]   40
Then he stamped the earth down flat around them.
Amazement gripped all those observing him,
to watch him organize those axes properly,
although before that time he'd never seen them.
Then, going and standing in the threshold, he tried
to test the bow. Three times he made it tremble,
as he strove to bend it, and three times he relaxed,
hoping in his heart he'd string that bow and shoot
an arrow through the iron. On his fourth attempt,
as his power bent the bow, he might have strung it,   50
but Odysseus shook his head, motioning him to stop,
for all his eagerness. So Telemachus spoke out,   [130]
addressing them once more with royal authority:

        "Well, I suppose I'll remain a coward,
    a weak man, too, in future days, or else
    I'm still too young and cannot yet rely
    on my own strength to guard me from a man
    who gets angry with me first. But come now,
    you men who are more powerful than me,
    test this bow. Let's end this competition."   60

Once he'd said this, Telemachus placed the bow
down on the ground away from him, leaning it
against the polished panels of the door, and set
a swift arrow there beside the bow's fine tip,
then sat down again in the chair from which he'd stood.
Then Antinous, Eupeithes' son, addressed them: [140]

        "All you comrades, get up in order now,
    from left to right, beginning from the place
    where the steward pours the wine."

---

[1]There has been some discussion about where this contest takes place. The most
obvious spot is the great hall itself, which has an earthen floor.

Antinous spoke,
and what he'd just proposed they found agreeable.   70
The first to stand up was Leiodes, son of Oenops,
their soothsayer. He always sat furthest away,
beside the lovely mixing bowl. That was the man
who first picked up the bow and the swift arrow.
After moving to the threshold and standing there,
he tried the bow, but couldn't string it. His hands,   [150]
which were delicate and weak, grew weary,
before he could succeed in stringing up the bow.
He then spoke out among the suitors:

"My friends,
I'm not the man to string this bow. So now,   80
let someone else take hold of it. This bow
will take away from many excellent men
their lives and spirits, since it's far better
to die than live and fail in the attempt
to have what we are gathered here to get,
always waiting here in hope day after day."

Then he sat again on the chair he'd risen from.
But Antinous took issue with what he'd just said,
talking directly to him:

"Leiodes,
what wretched, sorry words! As I listened,   90
it made me angry—as if this bow would,   [170]
in fact, take away the lives and spirits
of the very finest men, just because
you could not string it. Your royal mother
did not produce in you the sort of man
who has sufficient strength to draw a bow
and shoot an arrow. But some other men
among these noble suitors will soon string it."

This said, Antinous called out to Melanthius,
the goatherd:

"Come now, Melanthius,   100
light a fire in the hall. Set beside it
a large chair with a fleece across it.
And bring a hefty piece of fat—there's some
inside the house—so the young men here

can warm the bow and rub grease into it,
then test the bow and end this contest." [180]

When he'd said this, Melanthius quickly lit
a tireless fire. Then he brought a large chair up,
draped a fleece on it, and set it down beside the fire
and from inside the house fetched a large piece of fat. 110
Then the young men warmed the bow and tested it.
But they could not string it—whatever strength they had
was far too little. Antinous and godlike Eurymachus,
the suitors' leaders, still remained—the two of them,
with their abilities, were the finest men by far.

Now, the cattle herder and the keeper of the swine
belonging to godlike Odysseus had gone out,
both together, so lord Odysseus himself [190]
left the house to follow after them. And then,
when they had gone beyond the gates and courtyard, 120
he spoke, addressing them with reassuring words:

"You there, cattleman and swineherd, shall I
tell you something or keep it to myself?
My spirit tells me I should speak to you.
If Odysseus were to come back suddenly,
brought from somewhere by a god, would you two
be the sort of men who would defend him?
Would you support the suitors or Odysseus?
Answer as your heart and spirit prompt you."

Then the cattle herder answered him:

"O Father Zeus, 130 [200]
would that you might fulfil this very wish—
may that man come, and led on by some god.
Then you would know the kind of strength I have
and how my hands can show my power."

And then Eumaeus, too, made the same sort of prayer
to all the gods that wise Odysseus would come back
to his own home. Once Odysseus had clearly seen
how firm their minds were, he spoke to them again,
saying these words:

"Well, here I am in person—
after suffering much misfortune, I've come home, 140
back in the twentieth year to my own land.

Of those who work for me, I recognize
that you're the only two who want me back.
Among the rest, I've heard no one praying   [210]
that my return would bring me home again.
I'll tell you both how this is going to end—
and I'll speak the truth—if, on my behalf
some god will overcome those noble suitors,
I'll bring you each a wife, and I'll provide
possessions and a house built near my own.   150
Then you'll be my companions—and kinsmen
of Telemachus. Come, I'll show you something,
a sure sign, so you will clearly know it's me
and trust me in your hearts—here's the old scar
I got from a boar's white tusk, when I'd gone
to Parnassus with Autolycus' sons."   [220]

As he said this, Odysseus pulled aside his rags,
exposing the great scar. Once those two had seen it
and noted every detail, they threw their arms
around the wise Odysseus, burst into tears,   160
and welcomed him, kissing his head and shoulders.
Odysseus did the same—he kissed their heads and hands.
They would have kept on crying until sunset,
if Odysseus himself hadn't called a halt and said:

    "Stop these laments. Let's have no more crying.
    Someone might come out from the hall, see us,
    and tell the people in the house. Let's go in,
    one by one, not all together. I'll go first.   [230]
    You come later. And let's make this our sign.
    All those other men, the noble suitors,   170
    will not allow the quiver and the bow
    to be given to me. But, good Eumaeus,
    as you're carrying that bow through the house,
    put it in my hands, and tell the women
    to lock their room with bolts. Now, as for you,   [240]
    good Philoetius, I want you to lock
    the courtyard gates. Bolt and lash them shut.
    Do it quickly."

                            After he'd said this,
Odysseus went into the stately home and sat down
on the chair from which he'd risen. The two men,   180
godlike Odysseus' servants, then went in as well.

Eurymachus already had the bow in hand,
warming it here and there in the firelight.
But even doing that, he could not string it.
Then his noble heart gave out a mighty groan,
and he spoke to them directly—he was angry.

"It's too bad. I'm frustrated for myself
and for you all. I'm not that unhappy   [250]
about the marriage, though I am upset.
There are many more Achaean women—   190
some here in sea-girt Ithaca itself,
others in different cities. But if we are
so weak compared to godlike Odysseus
that we can't string his bow, it's a disgrace
which men will learn about in years to come."

Antinous, Eupeithes' son, then answered him:

"Eurymachus, that's not going to happen.
You yourself know it. At this moment,
in the country there's a feast day, sacred
to the god. So who would bend the bow? No,   200
set it to one side without saying anything.
So come, let the steward begin to pour
wine in the cups, so we can make libations.
Set the curved bow aside. In the morning,
we will test the bow and end the contest."

Antinous finished. Once they'd poured libations
and drunk wine to their heart's content, Odysseus,
a crafty man who had a trick in mind, spoke out:

"Suitors of the splendid queen, listen to me,
so I can say what the heart inside my chest   210
is prompting me to state. It's a request,
a plea, especially to Eurymachus
and godlike Antinous, since what he said
was most appropriate—that for the moment
you should stop this business with the bow
and turn the matter over to the gods.
In the morning a god will give the strength   [280]
to whoever he desires. But come now,
give me the polished bow, so here among you
I can test my power and arms and see   220
if I still have strength in my supple limbs

the way I used to have, or if my travels
and my lack of food have quite destroyed it."

Then Antinous, speaking to him directly,
took Odysseus to task:

                "You wretched stranger,
your mind lacks any sense—you've none at all.
Aren't you content to share a feast with us,
such illustrious men, without being disturbed   [290]
or lacking any food, and then to hear
what we say to one another as we speak?"   230 [310]

Wise Penelope then answered him and said:

    "Antinous, it's neither good nor proper
to deny guests of Telemachus a chance,
no matter who it is comes to this house.
And if, trusting in his strength and power,
the stranger strings Odysseus' great bow,
do you think he'll take me to his home
and make me his wife? I'm sure he himself
carries no such hope in that chest of his.
So none of you should be at dinner here   240
with sorrow in your heart because of him.
That would be undignified."

Shrewd Telemachus then answered her:

                "Mother,
among Achaeans, no man has a right
stronger than my own to give the bow
to anyone I wish or to withhold it—
none of those who rule in rocky Ithaca
or in the islands neighbouring Elis,
where horses graze. Among these men, no one
will deny my will by force, if I wish   250
to give the bow, even to this stranger,
as an outright gift to take away with him.
But you should go up to your own chamber   [350]
and keep busy with your proper work,
the loom and spindle, and tell your women
to go about their tasks. The bow will be
a matter for the men, especially me,
since the power in this house is mine."

Penelope, astonished, went back to her rooms,
taking to heart the prudent words her son had said.   260

The worthy swineherd had picked up the curving bow
and was carrying it. He came to shrewd Odysseus
and placed it in his hands. Then he called the nurse,   [380]
Eurycleia, and said to her:

         "Wise Eurycleia,
Telemachus is telling you to lock up
the closely fitted doorway to this hall.
If anyone hears groans inside this room
or any noise from men within these walls,
she's not to run outside, but stay where she is,
carrying out her work in silence."[1]   270

After he'd said this, her words could find no wings.
So she locked the doors of that well-furnished hall.
And Philoetius, without a word, slipped outside
and locked the courtyard gates, then went inside,
sat down again on the seat where he'd got up,
and observed Odysseus, who already had the bow.
He was turning it this way and that, testing it
in different ways to see if, while its lord was gone,
worms had nibbled on the horns. Shrewd Odysseus,
once he'd raised the bow and looked it over   280
on all sides, then—just as someone really skilled
at playing the lyre and singing has no trouble
when he loops a string around a brand-new peg,
tying the twisted sheep's gut down at either end—
that's how easily Odysseus strung that great bow.
Holding it in his right hand, he tried the string.   [410]
It sang out, resonating like a swallow's song,
beneath his touch. Grief overwhelmed the suitors.
Then he picked up a swift arrow lying by itself
on the table there beside him. He set it   290
against the bow, on the bridge, pulled the notched arrow
and the bow string back—still sitting in his seat—   [420]
and with a sure aim let the arrow fly. It did not miss,
not even a single top on all the axe heads.

---

[1]The doorway in question is the entrance to the women's quarters. They are to be
locked in so that they don't interrupt the revenge killings or run off to raise a
general alarm.

The arrow, weighted with bronze, went straight through
and out the other end. And then Odysseus
called out to Telemachus:

         "Telemachus, the stranger
sitting in your halls has not disgraced you.
I did not miss my aim or work too long
to string that bow. My strength is still intact,   300
in spite of all the suitors' scornful gibes.
Now it's time to get a dinner ready
for these Achaeans, while there's still some light,
then entertain ourselves in different ways,
with singing and the lyre. These are things   [430]
which should accompany a banquet."

As he spoke, he gave a signal with his eyebrows.
Telemachus, godlike Odysseus' dear son,
cinched up his sword, closed his fist around a spear,
moved close beside his father, right by his seat,   310
and stood there, fully armed with glittering bronze.

XXII
THE KILLING OF THE SUITORS

Then shrewd Odysseus stripped off his rags, grabbed up
the bow and quiver full of arrows, and sprang
over to the large doorway. He dumped swift arrows
right there at his feet and then addressed the suitors:

> "This competition to decide the issue
> is now over. But there's another target—
> one no man has ever struck—I'll find out
> if I can hit it. May Apollo grant
> I get the glory."

          As Odysseus spoke,
he aimed a bitter arrow straight at Antinous,   10
who was just about to raise up to his lips
a fine double-handled goblet he was holding   [10]
in his hands, so he could drink some wine. In his heart
there was no thought of slaughter. Among those feasting,
who would ever think in such a crowd of people,
one man, even with truly outstanding strength,
would bring himself an evil death, his own black fate?
Odysseus took aim and hit him with an arrow
in the throat. Its point passed through his tender neck.
He slumped onto his side, and, as he was hit,   20
the cup fell from his hand. A thick spurt of human blood
came flowing quickly from his nose. Then, suddenly
he pushed the table from him with his foot, spilling   [20]
food onto the floor—the bread and roasted meat
were ruined. When the suitors saw Antinous fall,
they raised an uproar. They began to shout,
yelling words of anger at Odysseus:

>   "Stranger,
> you'll pay for shooting arrows at this man.
> For you there'll be no contests any more.
> It's certain you'll be killed once and for all.   30
> You've killed a man, by far the finest youth
> in all of Ithaca. And now the vultures   [30]
> are going to eat you up right here."

          They did not think
he had killed the man on purpose. In their foolishness,
they did not realize they'd all become enmeshed

in destruction's snare. Shrewd Odysseus scowled at them
and gave his answer:

> "You dogs, because you thought
> I'd not come back from Troy to my own home,
> you've been ravaging my house, raping women,
> and in your devious way wooing my wife,   40
> while I was still alive, with no fear of the gods,
> who hold wide heaven, or of any man   [40]
> who might take his revenge in days to come.
> And now a fatal net has caught you all."

As Odysseus said these words, pale fear seized everyone.
Each man looked around to see how he might flee
complete destruction. Only Eurymachus spoke—
he answered him and said:

> "If, in fact, it's true
> that you're Odysseus of Ithaca,
> back home again, you're right in what you say   50
> about the actions of Achaeans here,
> their frequent reckless conduct in your home,
> their many foolish actions in the fields.
> But the man responsible for all these things
> now lies there dead—I mean Antinous.
> Now he himself has died, as he deserved.
> So at this point you should spare your people.
> Later on we'll collect throughout the land
> repayment for all we've had to eat and drink
> inside your halls, and every man will bring   60
> compensation on his own, in an amount
> worth twenty oxen, paying you back in gold
> and bronze until your heart is mollified."

> Shrewd Odysseus glared at him   [60]
and then replied:

> "Eurymachus, if you gave me
> all the goods you got from your own fathers,
> everything which you now own, and added
> other assets you could obtain elsewhere,
> not even then would I hold back my hands
> from slaughter, not until the suitors pay
> for all their arrogance. Now you've a choice—   70
> to fight here face to face or, if any man

wishes to evade his death and lethal fate,
to run away. But I don't think there's one
who will escape complete destruction."

Once Odysseus spoke, their knees and hearts went slack
right where they stood. Then Eurymachus spoke once more,
calling out to them:

        "Friends, this man won't hold in check   [70]
those all-conquering hands of his. Instead,
now he's got the polished bow and quiver,
from that smooth threshold he'll just shoot at us   80
until he's killed us all. So let's think now
about how we should fight. Pull out your swords,
and set tables up to block those arrows—
they bring on death so fast. And then let's charge,
go at him all together in a group."

With these words, Eurymachus pulled out his sword,
a sharp two-edged blade of bronze, and then charged out   [80]
straight at Odysseus, with a blood-curdling shout.
As he did so, lord Odysseus shot an arrow.
It struck him in the chest beside the nipple   90
and drove the swift shaft straight down into his liver.
Eurymachus' sword fell from his hand onto the ground.
He bent double and then fell, writhing on the table,
knocking food and two-handled cups onto the floor.
His forehead kept hammering the earth, his heart
in agony, as both his feet kicked at the chair
and made it shake. A mist fell over both his eyes.
Then Amphinomus went at glorious Odysseus,
charging straight for him. He'd drawn out his sharp sword,   [90]
to see if he would somehow yield the door to him.   100
But Telemachus moved in too quickly for him—
he threw a bronze-tipped spear and hit him from behind
between the shoulders. He drove it through his chest.
With a crash, Amphinomus fell, and his forehead
struck hard against the ground. Telemachus jumped back,
leaving his spear in Amphinomus, afraid that,
if he tried to pull out the long-shadowed spear,
some Achaean might attack and stab him with a sword
or strike him while he was stooping down. And so
he quickly ran away and then moved across   110

to his dear father. Standing close to him, he spoke—   [100]
his words had wings:

> "Father, now I'll bring you
> a shield, two spears, and a bronze helmet,
> one that fits your temples. When I get back,
> I'll arm myself and hand out other armour
> to the swineherd and the keeper of the goats.
> It's better if we fully arm ourselves."

Quick-witted Odysseus answered him and said:

> "Get them here fast, while still I have arrows
> to protect myself, in case they push me   120
> from the doors, since I'm here by myself."

Odysseus spoke, and Telemachus obeyed
his dear father. He went off to the storeroom
where their splendid weapons lay. From the place
he took four shields, eight spears, and four bronze helmets   [110]
with thick horsehair plumes. He went out carrying these
and came back to his dear father very quickly.
First he armed himself with bronze around his body,
and the two servants did the same, putting on
the lovely armour. Then they took their places   130
on either side of skilled and sly Odysseus,
who, as long as he had arrows to protect him,
kept on aiming at the suitors in his house,
shooting at them one by one. As he hit them,
they fell down in heaps. But once he'd used his arrows,
the king could shoot no more. So he leaned the bow   [120]
against the doorpost of the well-constructed wall,
and let it stand beside the shining entrance way.
Then on his own he set across his shoulders
his four-layered shield, and on his powerful head   140
he placed a beautifully crafted helmet
with horsehair nodding ominously on top.
Then he grabbed two heavy bronze-tipped spears.   [130]
Then Agelaus spoke, calling all the suitors:

> "Friends, can someone climb up to that side door
> and tell the men to raise a quick alarm?
> Then this man won't be shooting any more."

But Melanthius the goatherd answered him and said:

"It can't be done, divinely raised Agelaus.
The fine gate to the yard is awfully near,   150
and the passage entrance hard to get through.
One man could block the way for everyone,
if he were brave. But come, let me bring you
armour from the storeroom. You can put it on.
It's in the house, I think—there's nowhere else   [140]
Odysseus and his noble son could store
their weapons."[1]

           Once goatherd Melanthius said this,
he climbed a flight of stairs inside the palace,
up to Odysseus' storerooms. There he took twelve shields,
as many spears, as many helmets made of bronze   160
with bushy horsehair plumes. Once he'd made it back,
carrying the weapons, as quickly as he could
he gave them to the suitors. When Odysseus saw them
putting armour on and their hands brandishing
long spears, his knees and his fond heart went slack.
His task appeared enormous. He called out quickly   [150]
to Telemachus—his words had wings:

              "Telemachus,
it seems one of the women in the house
is stirring up a nasty fight against us,
or perhaps Melanthius might be the one."   170

Shrewd Telemachus then said in reply:

"Father, I bear the blame for this myself.
It's no one else's fault. I left it open—
the close-fitting door of that storage room.
One of them has keener eyes than I do.
Come, good Eumaeus, shut the storeroom door.
And try to learn if one of the women
has done this, or if it's Melanthius,
son of Dolius—I suspect it's him."

While they were saying these things to one another,   180 [160]
Melanthius the goatherd went back once more
to carry more fine armour from the storeroom.

---

[1] For a picture which illustrates the relative positions of the people inside the great hall, consult the diagram at the end of this book (p. 164-5).

But the loyal swineherd saw him and spoke out,
saying a quick word to Odysseus, who was close by:

> "Resourceful Odysseus, Laertes son,
> raised from Zeus, there's that man again,
> the wretch we think is visiting the storeroom.
> Give me clear instructions. Should I kill him,
> if I prove the stronger man, or should I
> bring him to you here? He can pay you back   190
> for the many insolent acts he's done,
> all those schemes he's thought up in your home."

Resourceful Odysseus then answered him and said: [170]

> "These proud suitors Telemachus and I
> will keep penned up here inside the hall,
> no matter how ferociously they fight.
> You two twist Melanthius' feet and arms
> behind him, throw him in the storeroom,
> then lash boards against his back. Tie the man
> to a twisted rope and then hoist him up   200
> the lofty pillar till he's near the beams.
> Let him stay alive a while and suffer
> in agonizing pain."

                    As Odysseus said this,
they listened eagerly and then obeyed his words.
They moved off to the storeroom, without being seen
by the man inside. He was, as it turned out, searching   [180]
for weapons in a corner of the room. So then,
when Melanthius the goatherd was coming out
across the threshold, the two men jumped out
and grabbed him. They dragged him inside by the hair,   210
threw him on the ground—the man was terrified—
and tied his feet and hands with heart-wrenching bonds.
They lashed them tight behind his back, as Odysseus,   [190]
Laertes' royal son, who had endured so much,
had told them. They fixed a twisted rope to him,
yanked him up the lofty pillar, and raised him
near the roof beams. They left Melanthius there,   [200]
tied up and hanging in bonds which would destroy him.
The two put on their armour, closed the shining door,
and made their way to wise and crafty Odysseus.   220
Filled with fighting spirit, they stood there, four of them
on the threshold, with many brave men in the hall.

The suitors were being urged on by Agelaus,
Damastor's son, by Eurynomus, Amphimedon,
Demoptolemus, Peisander, Polyctor's son,
and clever Polybus. Among the suitors still alive
these were the finest men by far. Odysseus' bow
and his swift arrows had destroyed the others.
Agelaus spoke to them, addressing everyone:

> "Friends, this man's hands have been invincible,   230
> but now they'll stop. Don't throw those spears at them,
> not all at once. Come, you six men throw first,
> to see if Zeus will let us strike Odysseus
> and win the glory. Those others over there
> will be no trouble after he's collapsed."

The suitors kept throwing spears with frantic haste,
but, though there were many, Athena made them miss.
One man struck the door post of the well-built hall.
Another hit the closely fitted door. One ash spear,
weighted down with bronze, fell against the wall.   240
But Amphimedon did hit Telemachus' hand
a glancing blow across the wrist. The bronze point
cut the surface of his skin. And with his long spear
Ctessipus grazed Eumaeus' shoulder above his shield,
but the spear veered off and fell down on the ground.   [280]
At close range Odysseus slaughtered Damastor's son
with his long spear, and Telemachus struck down
Leocritus, son of Evenor—he struck him
with his spear right in the groin and drove the bronze
straight through—so Leocritus fell on his face,   250
his whole forehead smashing down onto the ground.
Just as falcons with hooked talons and curved beaks
fly down from mountains, chasing birds and driving them
well below the clouds, as they swoop along the plain,
and then pounce and kill them, for there's no defence,
no flying away, while men get pleasure from the chase,
that's how Odysseus and his men pursued the suitors
and struck them down, one by one, throughout the hall.
As they smashed their heads in, dreadful groans arose,
and the whole floor was awash in blood.   260

And then the minstrel Phemius, son of Terpes,   [330]
who'd been compelled to sing before the suitors,
kept trying to get away from his own murky fate.

So he set the hollow lyre down on the ground, [340]
between the mixing bowl and silver-studded chair,
rushed out in person to clasp Odysseus' knees,
and pleaded with him—his words had wings:

> "I implore you, Odysseus, show me respect
> and pity. There'll be sorrow for you later,
> if you kill me, a minstrel, for I sing 270
> to gods and men. I am self-taught. The god
> has planted in my heart all kinds of songs,
> and I'm good enough to sing before you,
> as to a god. Don't be too eager then
> to cut my throat. Your dear son Telemachus [350]
> could tell you that it wasn't my desire
> nor did I need to spend time at your house,
> singing for the suitors at their banquets.
> But their greater power and numbers
> brought me here by force."

As Phemius said this, 280
royal Telemachus heard him and spoke up,
calling to his father, who was close by:

> "Hold on. Don't let your sword injure this man.
> He's innocent. We should save Medon, too,
> the herald, who always looked out for me
> inside the house when I was still a child,
> unless Philoetius has killed him,
> or the swineherd, or he ran into you
> as you were on the rampage in the hall." [360]

Telemachus spoke. Medon, whose mind was clever, 290
heard him, for he was cowering underneath a chair,
his skin covered by a new-flayed ox-hide, trying
to escape his own black fate. He quickly jumped out
from beneath the chair, threw off the ox-hide,
rushed up to clasp Telemachus' knees, and begged—
his words had wings:

> "Here I am, my friend.
> Stop! And tell your father to restrain himself,
> in case, as he exults in his great power,
> he slaughters me with that sharp bronze of his,
> in his fury with the suitors, those men 300

145

who consumed his goods here in his own hall, [370]
those fools who did not honour you at all."

Resourceful Odysseus then smiled at him and said:

"Cheer up! This man here has saved your life.
He's rescued you, so you know in your heart
and can tell someone else how doing good
is preferable by far to acting badly."

After Odysseus spoke, the two men went away,
outside the hall, and sat down there, by the altar
of great Zeus, peering round in all directions, 310 [380]
always thinking they'd be killed.

                 Odysseus, too,
looked round the house to check if anyone
was hiding there, still alive, trying to escape
his own dark fate. But every man he looked at—
and there were plenty—had fallen in blood and dust,
like fish which, in the meshes of a net, fishermen
have pulled from the grey sea up on the curving beach,
lying piled up on the sand, longing for sea waves,
while the bright sun takes away their life—that's how
the suitors then were lying in heaps on one another. 320
Resourceful Odysseus then said to Telemachus: [390]

"Telemachus, go and call the nurse in here,
Eurycleia, so I can speak to her.
Something's on my mind—I want to tell her."

Once Odysseus spoke, Telemachus obeyed
what his dear father said. He shook the door and called
to Eurycleia, saying:[1]

                "Get up, old woman,
born so long ago—the one in charge
of female servants in the palace.
Come out. My father's calling for you. 330
He's got something he wants to say."

He spoke. But Eurycleia's words could find no wings.
She opened up the door of the well-furnished hall

---

[1]The doorway here is the entrance to the women's quarters. At the start of the slaughter Eurycleia had locked it to prevent any of the women coming into the great hall or escaping to raise the alarm.

and came out. Telemachus went first and led the way.   [400]
There she found Odysseus with the bodies of the dead,
spattered with blood and gore, like a lion moving off
from feeding on a farmyard ox, his whole chest
and both sides of his muzzle caked with blood,
a terrifying sight, that's how Odysseus looked,
with bloodstained feet and upper arms. Eurycleia,   340
once she saw the bodies and huge amounts of blood,
was ready to cry out for joy now that she'd seen
such a mighty act. But Odysseus held her back
and checked her eagerness. He spoke to her—   [410]
his words had wings:

      "Old woman, you can rejoice
in your own heart—but don't cry out aloud.
Restrain yourself. For it's a sacrilege
to boast above the bodies of the slain.
Divine Fate and their own reckless acts
have killed these men, who failed to honour   350
any man on earth who came among them,
bad or good. And so through their depravity
they've met an evil fate. But come now,
tell me about the women in these halls,
the ones who disrespect me and the ones
who bear no blame."

      His dear nurse Eurycleia
then answered him and said:

      "All right my child,   [420]
I'll tell you the truth. In these halls of yours,
there are fifty female servants, women
we have taught to carry out their work,   360
to comb out wool and bear their slavery.
Of these, twelve in all have gone along
without a sense of shame and no respect
for me or even for Penelope herself."

      Resourceful Odysseus   [430]
then answered her:

      "Those women who before all this
behaved so badly, tell them to come here."

Odysseus then called Telemachus to him,
together with Eumaeus and Philoetius.
He spoke to them—his words had wings:

> "Start carrying those corpses outside now,   370
> and then take charge of the servant women.
> Have these splendid chairs and tables cleaned,
> wiped with porous sponges soaked in water.
> Once you've put the entire house in order,   [440]
> then take those servants from the well-built hall
> to a spot outside between the round house
> and the sturdy courtyard wall and kill them.
> Slash them with long swords, until the life is gone
> from all of them, and they've forgotten
> Aphrodite and how they loved the suitors   380
> when they had sex with them in secret."

Odysseus spoke. Then the crowd of women came,
wailing plaintively and shedding many tears.
First they gathered up the corpses of the dead
and laid them out underneath the portico,
leaning them against each other in the well-fenced yard.   [450]
Odysseus himself gave them their instructions
and hurried on the work. The women were compelled
to carry out the dead. After that, they cleaned
the splendid chairs and tables, wiping them down   390
with water and porous sponges. Telemachus,
along with Philoetius and Eumaeus,
with shovels scraped the floor inside the well-built hall,
and women took the dirt and threw it in the yard.
When they'd put the entire hall in order,
they led the women out of the sturdy house
to a place between the round house and fine wall
around the courtyard, herding them into a narrow space   [460]
where there was no way to escape. Shrewd Telemachus
began by speaking to the other two:

> "I don't want   400
> to take these women's lives with a clean death.
> They've poured insults on my head, on my mother,
> and were always sleeping with the suitors."

He spoke, then tied the cable of a dark-prowed ship
to a large pillar, threw one end above the round house,
then pulled it taut and high, so no woman's foot

could reach the ground.[1] Just as doves or long-winged thrushes
charge into a snare set in a thicket, as they seek out
their roosting place, and find out they've been welcomed   [470]
by a dreadful bed, that's how those women held their head   410
all in a row, with nooses fixed around their necks,
so they'd have a pitiful death. For a little while
they twitched their feet, but that did not last long.
Then they brought Melanthius out through the doorway
into the yard. With pitiless bronze they sliced away
his nose and ears, then ripped off his cock and balls
as raw meat for dogs to eat, and in their rage
hacked off his hands and feet. After they'd done that,
they washed their hands and feet and went inside the house,
back to Odysseus. Their work was done. But he   420 [480]
called out to Eurycleia, his dear nurse:

                "Old woman,
  bring sulphur here to purify the house.
  And bring me fire so I can purge the hall.
  Ask Penelope to come here with her slaves,
  and get all the women in the house to come."

Dear nurse Eurycleia then followed what he'd said.
She brought fire and sulphur, so Odysseus
purged the house and yard completely. Eurycleia
went back through Odysseus' splendid home to tell
the women what had happened and to order them   430
to reappear. They came out holding torches,
then gathered round Odysseus, embracing him.
They clasped and kissed his head, his hands, and shoulders,
in loving welcome. A sweet longing seized him   [500]
to sigh and weep, for in his heart he knew them all.

---

[1] The round house is in one corner of the courtyard. Telemachus hangs the servant
women from a cable attached to the top of the round house and to a nearby pillar.

XXIII
ODYSSEUS AND PENELOPE

Old Eurycleia went up to an upstairs room,
laughing to herself, to inform her mistress
her beloved husband was inside the house.
She stood beside her lady's head and spoke to her:

> "Wake up, Penelope, my dear child,
> so you can see for yourself with your own eyes
> what you've been wanting each and every day.
> Odysseus has arrived. He may be late,
> but he's back in the house. And he's killed
> those arrogant suitors who upset this home,   10
> used up his goods, and victimized his son."

Penelope rejoiced. She jumped up out of bed,
hugged the old woman, tears falling from her eyelids,
then she spoke to her—her words had wings:

> "Come now,
> dear nurse, tell me the truth. If he's really here,
> back home as you claim, then how could he
> turn his hands against those shameless suitors?
> He was alone, and in this house those men
> were always in a group."

> Her dear nurse Eurycleia
then answered her:

> "I didn't see or hear about it.   20   [40]
> I only heard the groans of men being killed.
> I found Odysseus standing with the bodies—
> dead men on the hard earth all around him,
> lying on each other, a heart-warming sight—
> and he was there, covered with blood and gore,
> just like a lion. Now, come along with me,
> so you two can be happy in your hearts.
> You've been through so much misfortune, and now
> what you've been looking forward to so long
> has come about at last. He's come himself,   30
> to his own hearth while still alive—he's found
> you and your son inside these halls and taken
> his revenge on all suitors in his home,
> men who acted harmfully against him."

Wise Penelope then answered Eurycleia:

"But this story can't be true, not the way
you've told it. One of the immortal gods
has killed the noble suitors out of rage
at their heart-rending pride and wicked acts.
They've met disaster through their foolishness.   40
But in some place far away Odysseus
has forfeited his journey to Achaea,
and he himself is lost. You find it hard
to grasp the plans of the eternal gods,
even though you're really shrewd. But let's go
to my son, so I can see the suitors
now they're dead—and the man who killed them."

Penelope spoke, then went down from the upper room.
Crossing the stone threshold, she went in the hall
and sat down in the firelight opposite Odysseus,   50
beside the further wall. He was sitting there   [90]
by a tall pillar, looking at the ground, waiting
to learn if his noble wife would speak to him
when her own eyes caught sight of him. She sat there
a long time in silence. Amazement gripped her heart—
sometimes her eyes gazed at him full in the face,
but other times she failed to recognize him,
he had such shabby clothing covering his body.
Telemachus spoke up, addressing a rebuke
directly to her:

      "Mother, you're a cruel woman,   60
with an unfeeling heart. Why turn aside
from my father in this way? Why not sit
over there, close to him, ask him questions?
No other woman's heart would be so hard   [100]
to make her keep her distance from a husband
who's come home to her in his native land
in the twentieth year, after going through
so many harsh ordeals. That heart of yours
is always harder than a stone."

              Wise Penelope
then answered him:

      "My child, inside my chest   70
my heart is quite amazed. I cannot speak

or ask questions, or look directly at him.
If indeed it's true he is Odysseus
and is home again, surely the two of us
have more certain ways to know each other.
We have signs only we two understand.   [110]
Other people will not recognize them."

As she spoke, lord Odysseus, who'd been through so much,
smiled and quickly spoke out to Telemachus—
his words had wings:

        "Telemachus, let your mother   80
test me in these halls. She will soon possess
more certain knowledge. Right now I'm filthy,
with disgusting clothing on my body.
That's why she rejects me and will not say
I am Odysseus."

        Once he said this, Eurynome,
the housekeeper, gave brave Odysseus a bath,
rubbed him with oil, and put a tunic on him,
a fine cloak, as well. Athena poured beauty on him
in large amounts to make him taller, more robust
to look at, and on his head she made his hair   90
flow in curls resembling a hyacinth in bloom.
He sat back down in the chair from which he'd risen,
opposite his wife, and said to her:

        "Strange lady,
to you those who live on Mount Olympus
have given, more so than to other women,
an unfeeling heart. No other woman
would harden herself and keep her distance
from her husband, who, in the twentieth year,
came back to her in his own native land,   [170]
after going through so much misfortune.   100
So come, nurse, spread out a bed for me,
so I can lie down by myself. The heart
inside her breast is made of iron."

Wise Penelope then answered him:

        "Strange man,
I am not making too much of myself
or ignoring you. Nor is it the case
that I'm particularly offended.

I know well the sort of man you were
when you left Ithaca in your long-oared ship.
So come, Eurycleia, set up for him   110
outside the well-built bedroom that strong bed
he made himself. Put that sturdy bedstead
out there for him and throw some bedding on,
fleeces, cloaks, and shining coverlets."   [180]

Penelope had said this to test her husband.
But Odysseus, angry at his true-hearted wife,
spoke out:

    "Woman, those words you've just said
are very painful. Who's shifted my bed
to some other place? That would be difficult,
even for someone really skilled, unless   120
a god came down in person—for he could,
if he wished, set it elsewhere easily.
But among men there is no one living,
no matter how much energy he has,
who would find it easy to shift that bed.
For built into the well-constructed bedstead
is a great symbol which I made myself
with no one else. A long-leaved olive bush   [190]
was growing in the yard. It was in bloom
and flourishing—it looked like a pillar.   130
I built my bedroom round this olive bush,
till I had finished it with well-set stones.
I put a good roof over it, then added
closely fitted jointed doors. After that,
I cut back the foliage, by removing
branches from the long-leaved olive bush.
I trimmed the trunk off, upward from the root,
cutting it skilfully and well with bronze,
so it followed a straight line. Once I'd made
the bedpost, I used an augur to bore out   140
the entire piece. That was how I started.
Then I carved out my bed, till I was done.
In it I set an inlay made of gold,   [200]
silver, and ivory, and then across it
I stretched a bright purple thong of ox-hide.
And that's the symbol I describe for you.
But, lady, I don't know if that bed of mine
is still in place or if some other man

has cut that olive tree down at its base
and set the bed up in a different spot." 150

Odysseus spoke, and sitting there, Penelope
went weak at the knees, and her heart grew soft.
For she recognized that it was true—that symbol
Odysseus had described to her. Eyes full of tears,
she ran to him, threw her arms around his neck,
kissed his head, and said:

        "Don't be angry, Odysseus,
not with me. In all other matters
you've been the cleverest of men. The gods [210]
have brought us sorrows—they were not willing
the two of us should stay beside each other 160
to enjoy our youth and reach together
the threshold of old age. Now's not the time
to rage at me, resenting what I've done
because I didn't welcome you this way
when I first saw you. For there are many men
who dream up wicked schemes. Argive Helen,
a child of Zeus, would never have had sex
with a man who came from somewhere else,
if she'd known Achaea's warrior sons [220]
would bring her back to her dear native land. 170
And some god drove her to that shameful act.
But now you've mentioned that clear symbol,
our bed, which no one else has ever seen,
other than the two of us, you and me,
and a single servant woman, Actoris,
whom my father gave me when I came here.
For both of us she kept watch at the doors
of our strong bedroom. You've now won my heart, [230]
though it's been truly stubborn."

                Penelope spoke
and stirred in him an even more intense desire 180
to weep. As he held his loyal and loving wife,
he cried. And rose-fingered early Dawn
would have appeared with them still weeping there,
if goddess Athena with the gleaming eyes,
had not thought of something else—she prolonged
the lengthy night as it came to an end, keeping
Dawn and her golden throne waiting by Ocean's stream.

While they went on talking to each other in this way,
Eurynome and the nurse prepared the bed
with soft coverlets, by light from flaming torches.   190   [290]
Once they'd quickly covered up the sturdy bed,
the old nurse went back to her room to rest,
and the bedroom servant, Eurynome, led them
on their way to bed, a torch gripped in her hands.
When she'd brought them to the room, then she returned.
Odysseus and Penelope approached with joy
the place where their bed stood from earlier days.

Odysseus and Penelope, once they'd had the joy   [300]
of making love, then entertained each other
telling stories, in mutual conversation.   200
The lovely lady talked of all she had been through
in the house, looking at that destructive group,
the suitors, who, because of her, had butchered
so many cattle and fat sheep and drained from jars
so much wine. Odysseus, born from Zeus, then told
all the troubles he'd brought down on men, all the grief
he had to work through on his own. Penelope
was happy listening, and sleep did not come down
across her eyelids until he had told it all.

Then Athena, goddess with the gleaming eyes,   210
came up with something else. When she thought Odysseus
had had his heart's fill of pleasure with his wife and slept,
from Ocean she quickly stirred up early Dawn
on her golden throne to bring her light to men.
Odysseus rose from his soft bed and told his wife:

    "Now that we've come back to the bed we love,
you should tend to our wealth inside the house.
As for flocks those arrogant suitors stole,
I'll seize many beasts as plunder on my own,
and Achaeans will give others, till they fill up   220
each and every pen. Now I'm going to go
out to my forest lands, and there I'll see
my noble father, who on my behalf   [360]
has suffered such anxiety. Lady,
since I know how intelligent you are,
I'm asking you to follow these instructions—
once sunrise comes, the story will be out
about the suitors slaughtered in our home.

So you should go up to your upper room
with your female attendants. Then sit there.   230
Don't look in on anyone or ask questions."

Once he'd said this, he put his lovely armour on,
around his shoulders, and roused Telemachus,
Philoetius, and Eumaeus, and told them all
to get weapons in their hands to fight a war.
They did not disobey, but dressed themselves in bronze,
opened the doors, and went outside, with Odysseus   [370]
in the lead. By now light was shining on the ground,
but Athena kept them hidden by the night,
as she led them quickly from the city.   240

XXIV

ZEUS AND ATHENA END THE FIGHTING

Once Odysseus and his men had left the city,
they soon reached Laertes' fine, well-managed farm,
which Laertes had once won by his own efforts,
working really hard. His house was there, with sheds
surrounding it on every side, where his servants,
bonded slaves who worked to carry out his wishes,   [210]
ate and sat and slept. An old Sicilian woman
lived inside his house, looking after the old man,
caring for him at the farm, far from the city.
Odysseus then spoke to his servants and his son: 10

"You should go inside the well-built home.
Hurry up and kill the finest pig there is,
so we can eat. I'll sound out my father,
to find out if he can recognize me,
see who I am, once he's laid eyes on me,
or if he doesn't know me any more,
since I've been away so long."

                              Odysseus spoke,
then gave his battle weapons to his servants.
In the well-established vineyard he found his father.
He was digging around a plant, all by himself,   20
dressed in a filthy, shabby, patched-up tunic.
Around his legs he'd tied shin pads stitched from ox-hide
to protect himself from scratches, and on his hands   [230]
he wore gloves, since there were thistles in that spot.
On his head he wore a goatskin hat. In these clothes
he was dealing with his grief. He stirred Odysseus' heart.
Already, as he looked at his dear father, sharp pains
were shooting up his nostrils. He jumped over,
embraced Laertes, kissed him, and then said: [320]

                              "Father,
I'm here—the very man you asked about.   30
I've returned here in the twentieth year,
back to my native land. Stop your grieving,
these tearful moans. I'll tell you everything,
though it's essential we move really fast.
I've killed the suitors in our home, avenged
their heart-rending insolence, their evil acts."

157

Laertes then answered him and said:

"If that's true,
if you are indeed my son Odysseus
and have come back, show me some evidence,
something clear so I can be quite certain."   40

Resourceful Odysseus replied to him and said: [330]

"First, let your eyes inspect this scar—a boar
inflicted that on me with its white tusk,
when I went to Parnassus, sent there
by you and by my honourable mother,
to her cherished father, Autolycus,
so I could get the gifts he'd promised me,
what he'd agreed to give when he was here."

As Odysseus spoke, his father's fond heart and knees
gave way—he clearly recognized the evidence   50
Odysseus had presented. He threw both his arms
around the son he loved and struggled hard to breathe.
Lord Odysseus, who had endured so much, held him.
After he'd revived and his spirit came once more
into his chest, Laertes spoke again and said: [350]

"Father Zeus, it seems you gods are still
on high Olympus, if it's true those suitors
have paid the price of their proud arrogance.
But now my heart contains a dreadful fear—
all the men of Ithaca will soon come here   60
against us, and they'll send out messengers
all through Cephallenia, to every city."[1]

Resourceful Odysseus then answered him and said:

"Take courage, and don't allow these things
to weigh down your heart. Let's go to the house,
the one close to the orchard, where I sent
Telemachus, together with the swineherd
and the keeper of the goats, so they could
prepare a meal as soon as possible."   [360]

After they'd talked like this, they went to the fine house.   70
Once they reached Laertes' well-furnished home, they found

---

[1]Cephallenia is the name of an island but is also used to refer to Odysseus' kingdom generally.

Telemachus with the swineherd and goat keeper
carving lots of meat and mixing gleaming wine.
Meanwhile, the other men had finished working.
Dinner was prepared. So they sat down one by one
on stools and chairs. As they were reaching for the food,
old Dolius appeared. The old man's sons were with him,
tired out from work. The ancient Sicilian woman,
their mother, had gone outside and summoned them.
Dolius went straight up to him, both arms outstretched,   80
grabbed Odysseus' hand and kissed it on the wrist.
Then he spoke to him—his words had wings:

                              "My friend,   [400]
    you're back with us, who longed for your return
    but never thought to see it! The gods themselves
    must have been leading you. Joyful greetings!
    May gods grant you success!"

                    Then Dolius' sons
also came up around glorious Odysseus,
clasping his hands.

                    Meanwhile, Rumour the Messenger
sped swiftly through the entire city, speaking
of the suitors' dreadful death, their destiny.   90
People heard about it all at once and came in
from all directions, gathering with mournful groans
before Odysseus' home. Each one brought his dead
outside the house and buried them. All the men
from other cities they sent home, placing them
aboard swift ships to be escorted back by sailors.
Then, with sorrowful hearts, they went in person   [420]
to meet in an assembly. Once they'd got there
together in a group, Eupeithes rose to speak.
Constant grief lay on his heart for his own son,   100
Antinous, the first man killed by lord Odysseus.
Weeping for him, he spoke to the assembly:

    "My friends, this man has planned and carried out
    dreadful acts against Achaeans. He led
    many fine courageous men off in his fleet,
    then lost his hollow ships, with all men dead.
    Now he's come and killed our finest men by far
    among the Cephallenians. So come on,
    before he can slip quickly off to Pylos   [430]

159

or to holy Elis, where Epeians rule,   110
let's get started. If not, in future days
we'll be eternally disgraced, since men
yet to be born will learn about our shame,
if we don't act to take out our revenge
on those murderers of our sons and brothers.
As far as I'm concerned, the life we'd live
would not be sweet. I'd rather die right now
and live among the dead. So let us go,
in case those men have a head start on us
and get across the sea."

         As Eupeithes said this,   120
he wept, and all Achaeans were seized by pity.
Then Medon and the godlike singer, released
from sleep, approached them from Odysseus' house   [440]
and stood up in their midst. They were astonished.
Then Medon, a shrewd man, spoke out.

         "Men of Ithaca,
now hear me. Odysseus did not plan these acts
without the gods' consent. I myself observed
an immortal god who stood beside him,
looking in every detail just like Mentor.
The deathless god appeared before Odysseus   130
at that time to spur him on to action,
and, at another time, charged through the hall,
terrifying the suitors. They collapsed in droves."

He ended. Some men stayed together in their seats,
but others, more than half, jumped up with noisy shouts.
Their hearts had not responded to what Medon said.
They'd been won over by Eupeithes. And so,
they quickly rushed away to get their weapons.

Then Athena spoke to Zeus, Cronos' son, saying:

        "Son of Cronos and Father of us all,   140
highest of all those who rule, answer me
when I ask this—What are you concealing
in that mind of yours? Will you be creating
further brutal war and dreadful battle,
or bring both sides together here as friends?"

Cloud-gatherer Zeus then answered her and said:

"My child, why are you asking this of me?
Why these questions? Were you not the one
who devised this plan all on your own,
so Odysseus could take out his revenge   150   [480]
against these men, after he got back?
Do as you wish. But I'll lay out for you
what I think is right. Since lord Odysseus
has paid back the suitors, let them swear
a binding oath that he'll remain their king
all his life, and let's make them forget
the killing of their sons and brothers.
Let them love each other as they used to do,
and let there be wealth and peace in plenty."

His words stirred up Athena, who was already keen.   160
She swooped down from the heights of Mount Olympus.

Meanwhile, once his group had eaten their hearts' fill
of food as sweet as honey, lord Odysseus,   [490]
who had endured so much, was the first to speak:

> "Someone should go outside to look around,
> see whether they are getting close to us."

Once he said this, a son of Dolius went out,
as he had ordered. He stood in the doorway
and saw all those men approaching. At once
he called out to Odysseus—his words had wings: 170

> "They're here, close by. Let's get our weapons—
> we'd better hurry!"

                              At these words, they leapt up
and put on their armour. Odysseus and his men
were four, the sons of Dolius six, and with them
Dolius and Laertes, though they had grey hair,
were dressed in armour, too, forced to be warriors.
When they'd put glittering bronze around their bodies,   [500]
they opened up the doors and went outside. Odysseus
led them out. But then Athena, Zeus' daughter,
with the shape and voice of Mentor, came up to them.   180
stood by Laertes, and said to him:

> "Child of Arcesius,
> by far the dearest of all those I cherish,
> pray to the young girl with the flashing eyes

161

and to Father Zeus, then without delay
raise that long spear of yours and throw it."

Pallas Athena spoke and then breathed into him   [520]
enormous power. Laertes said a prayer
to great Zeus' daughter, and quickly lifting up
his long-shadowed spear, he threw it. It hit home,
through the bronze cheek piece on Eupeithes' helmet,   190
which didn't stop the spear—the bronze point went on through.
Eupeithes fell down with a thud, his armour
crashing round him. Odysseus and his splendid son
charged at the fighters in the front, striking them
with swords and two-edged spears. They'd have killed them all,
cut them down so none of them returned, had not
Athena, daughter of aegis-bearing Zeus, cried out—
her voice held back every man in that whole army.   [530]

   "Men of Ithaca, stop this disastrous war,
   so you can quickly go your separate ways   200
   without spilling any blood."

                              Athena spoke,
and pale fear gripped the men. They were so terrified
they dropped their weapons and all fell on the ground,
at that goddess' resounding voice. They turned round,
back towards the city, eager to save their lives.
Then much-enduring lord Odysseus gave out
a fearful shout, gathered himself, and swooped down
like an eagle from on high. But at that moment,
Zeus, son of Cronos, shot a fiery thunderbolt.
It struck at the feet of the bright-eyed daughter   210 [540]
of that mighty father. And then Athena,
goddess with the glittering eyes, said to Odysseus:

   "Resourceful Odysseus, Laertes' son,
   and child of Zeus, hold back. Stop this fight,
   this impartial war, in case thundering Zeus,
   who sees far and wide, grows angry with you."

Once Athena spoke, Odysseus obeyed,
joy in his heart. And then Pallas Athena,
daughter of aegis-bearing Zeus, in shape and form
looking just like Mentor, had both parties swear   220
a solemn treaty designed to last forever.

APPENDICES

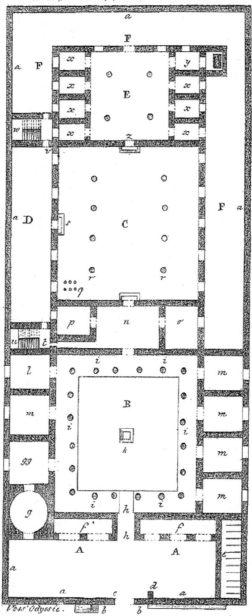

ODYSSEUS' PALACE, ACCORDING TO VOSS (1820)
(used with permission of Carlos Parada of the Greek Mythology Link)

DESCRIPTION OF LETTERS ON DIAGRAM

The following labels refer to the diagram on the facing page:

a. the outer wall

b. the entrance

c. the gates

e. standing place for mules

f. two halls

g. the dome

h. the entrance to the court

i. the hall

k. Zeus' altar in the court

l. Telemachus' room

m. various rooms

n. vestibule

o. room for bathing

p. activity room

q. wine preparation room

r. pillars

s. simple doors

t. door from vestibule

u. stair to Odysseus' rooms

v. door to women's rooms

w. stairs to Penelope's room

x. ground floor rooms

y. Penelope's bedroom

z. door.

A. courtyard and fence

B. level middle court

C. the hall

D. passage by-passing the hall

E. Penelope's work room

F. rear courtyard

When Odysseus kills the Suitors he is standing with his bow at the lower entrance to the main hall, C. The doors to the women's quarters (at v and z) have been locked. The only way out for the Suitors is a small door at s, which leads to the passageway D. Odysseus places Eumaeus at the end of the passage (at point t) to prevent any Suitor getting out into the courtyard B.

GLOSSARY OF NAMES

The following glossary includes the names of the main characters and places in the *Abridged Odyssey* and a few others.

ACHAEANS: a collective name of the Greeks (used interchangeably with DANAANS and ARGIVES)

ACHILLES: son of Peleus, greatest of the Achaean warriors at Troy, where he died and was buried.

AEGISTHUS: son of Thyestes, lover of Clytaemnestra and murderer of Agamemnon.

AEOLUS: son of Hippotas, god of the winds, living on the island Aeolia.

AGAMEMNON: son of Atreus, king of Argos, leader of the Achaean forces which attacked and destroyed Troy.

AGELAUS: son of Damastor, one of the Suitors.

AJAX: son of Telamon, greatest Achaean warrior after Achilles at Troy, where he died and was buried.

ALCINOUS: king of the Phaeacians, husband of Arete.

AMPHIMEDON: son of Melaneus, one of the Suitors.

AMPHINOMUS: son of Nisus, one of the Suitors from Dulichium.

AMPHITRITE: divine wife of Poseidon, a sea goddess.

ANTICLEIA: daughter of Autolycus, mother of Odysseus.

ANTINOUS: son of Eupeithes, one of the leaders of the Suitors.

ANTIPHATES: king of the Laestrygonians.

APOLLO: son of Zeus and Leto, often called Phoebus or Phoebus Apollo.

ARCESIUS: father of Laertes and thus Odysseus' grandfather.

ARETE: wife of Alcinous, queen of the Phaeacians.

ARGIVES: see ACHAEANS.

ARTEMIS: divine daughter of Zeus and Leto, goddess of the hunt.

ATHENA: divine daughter of Zeus, goddess of wisdom.

ATREUS: father of Agamemnon and Menelaus, who are often called "sons of Atreus."

CALYPSO: goddess living on the island of Ogygia.

CHARYBDIS: a divine sea monster which acts as a whirlpool.

CICONES: inhabitants of Ismarus, a city close to Troy.

CIRCE: a goddess living on the island of Aeaea.

CYCLOPES (singular CYCLOPS): monstrous creatures with one eye.

CRONOS: father of Zeus, overthrown by his son and imprisoned deep in the earth.

DANAANS: see ACHAEANS.

DEMODOCUS: the blind minstrel in the court of Phaeacia.

DOLIUS: an old servant of Laertes and Penelope.

DULICHIUM: an island close to Ithaca, part of Odysseus' kingdom.

EUMAEUS: a servant of Odysseus, keeper of pigs.

EUPEITHES: father of Antinous (one of the Suitors).

EURYCLEIA: old servant to Odysseus, Penelope, and Telemachus.

EURYMACHUS: son of Polybus, one of the leading Suitors.

EURYNOME: housekeeper in Odysseus' and Penelope's home.

FURIES: goddesses of blood revenge, especially within the family.

HADES: god of the underworld, also the underworld itself.

HELIOS: see HYPERION

HEPHAESTUS: divine son of Zeus and Hera, god of the forge, divine artisan.

HERCULES: mortal son of Zeus, made into a god after his death.

HERMES: divine son of Zeus and the nymph Maia, messenger god, often called "killer of Argus."

HYPERION: god of the sun (also called HELIOS).

ILION: another name for TROY.

ITHACA: island off the west coast of mainland Greece, kingdom ruled by Odysseus.

LACEDAEMONIA: a region in the central Peloponnese surrounding SPARTA. The names are often used interchangeably.

LAERTES: son of Arcesius, father of Odysseus.

LAESTRYGONIANS: race of giants living in Telpylus.

LEIODES: son of Oenops, one of the Suitors, a soothsayer.

LEOCRITUS: son of Euenor, one of the Suitors.

MEDON: a herald in Odysseus' palace.

MELANTHIUS: son of Dolius, a goatherd friendly to the Suitors.

MENELAUS: son of Atreus, brother of Agamemnon, husband of Helen, king of Sparta.

MENTOR: steward of Odysseus' place, a companion of Odysseus.

NAUSICAA: daughter of Arete, young princess of the Phaeacians.

NERITON: a mountain in Ithaca.

NESTOR: king of Pylos.

NOEMON: son of Phronius, a friend of Telemachus in Ithaca.

OCEANUS: the river running around the outer rim of the world.

ODYSSEUS: king of Ithaca, son of Laertes, husband of Penelope, father of Telemachus.

OLYMPUS: mountain in northern Greece where the major deities live (the Olympians).

OGYGIA: island where Calypso lives, where she detains Odysseus.

ORESTES: son of Agamemnon, killer of Aegisthus.

PENELOPE: wife of Odysseus, mother of Telemachus, daughter of Icarius.

PERSEPHONE: wife of Hades, goddess of the underworld.

PHAEACIANS: inhabitants of Scheria, master sailors.

PHEMIUS: son of Terpes, the professional minstrel in Odysseus' palace.

PHILOETIUS: a goat and cattle herder friendly to Odysseus.

POLYPHEMUS: a cyclops, son of Poseidon.

PONTONOUS: a herald in the court of Alcinous in Phaeacia.

POSEIDON: god of the sea, brother of Zeus, often called "shaker of the earth" or "Earthshaker."

PRIAM: king of Troy, killed when the city was captured and destroyed by Achaeans.

PYLOS: city state in the south Peloponnese ruled by Nestor.

PYTHO: the location of the shrine of Apollo.

SAME: an island close to Ithaca, part of Odysseus' kingdom.

SCHERIA: distant land where the Phaeacians live.

SCYLLA: a monster with six heads.

SIRENS: two singers who lure sailors to their destruction.

SPARTA: city in the central Peloponnese ruled by Menelaus.

STYX: river in Hades by which the gods swear their most solemn oaths.

SUITORS: aristocratic young men courting Penelope in hopes of marrying her.

TAPHIANS: inhabitants of some islands close to Ithaca.

TEIRESIAS: a blind prophet from Thebes, now in Hades.

TELEMACHUS: son of Odysseus and Penelope.

TROY: city in Asia Minor, near the Hellespont, besieged by the Achaean (Greek) forces for ten years. Also called ILION.

ZACYNTHUS: an island close to Ithaca, part of Odysseus' kingdom.

ZEUS: major divine presence on Olympus, father of numerous gods and goddesses, often called "son of Cronos."

Ancient Greece and the Eastern Mediterranean

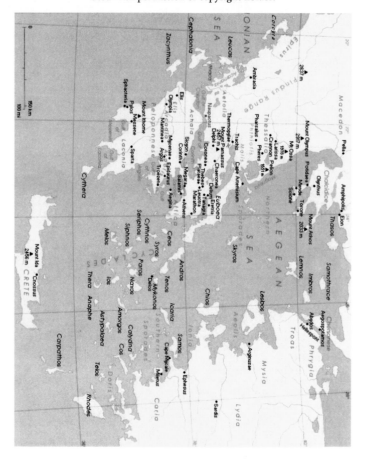

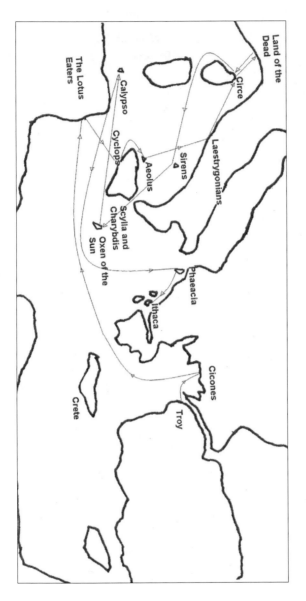

One Possible Representation of Odysseus' Journey Home.
The most questionable location is Calypso's island, which may be
further west or in the east.

Ian Johnston is an emeritus professor at Vancouver Island University, Nanaimo, British Columbia, Canada. He is the author of *The Ironies of War: An Introduction to Homer's Iliad* and has translated a number of classic works into English, including the following (most of them published as books and ebooks by Richer Resources Publications).

Aeschylus, *Oresteia*
Aeschylus, *Persians*
Aeschylus, *Prometheus Bound*
Aeschylus, *Seven Against Thebes*
Aeschylus, *Suppliant Women*
Aristophanes, *Birds*
Aristophanes, *Clouds*
Aristophanes, *Frogs*
Aristophanes, *Knights*
Aristophanes, *Lysistrata*
Aristophanes, *Peace*
Cuvier, *Discourse on Revolutionary Upheavals on the Surface of the Earth*
Descartes, *Discourse on Method*
Descartes, *Meditations on First Philosophy*
Diderot, *D'Alembert's Dream and Rameau's Nephew*
Euripides, *Bacchae*
Euripides, *Electra*
Euripides *Hippolytus*
Euripides, *Medea*
Euripides, *Orestes*
Homer, *Iliad*
Homer, *Odyssey*
Kafka, *Metamorphosis, A Hunger Artist, In the Penal Colony, and Other Stories*
Kant, *On Perpetual Peace*
Kant, *Universal History and Nature of the Heavens*
Lamarck, *Zoological Philosophy, Volume I*
Lucretius, *On the Nature of Things*
Nietzsche, *Birth of Tragedy*
Nietzsche, *Beyond Good and Evil*
Nietzsche, *Genealogy of Morals*
Nietzsche, *On the Uses and Abuses of History*
Ovid, *Metamorphoses*
Rousseau, *Discourse on the Sciences and the Arts*
Rousseau, *Discourse on the Origins of Inequality*
Rousseau, *Social Contract*
Sophocles, *Ajax*
Sophocles, *Antigone*
Sophocles, *Oedipus the King*
Sophocles, *Oedipus at Colonus*
Sophocles, *Philoctetes*

Ian Johnston has a web site (at http://records.viu.ca/~johnstoi/) where he has posted these translations, as well as a number of lectures, workbooks, essays, and book reviews.